M000190432

# SHE STOLE MY

# HR

# PROMOTION!

**An Unforgettable Story About
Not Getting Promoted In Human Resources
& THE NUMBER <u>ONE</u> SUCCESS SECRET
For Advancing Your HR Career Faster And
Easier Than You Thought Possible!**

# Alan Collins
# Allison Quinn

Success in HR Publishing
Chicago, Illinois USA

*For those in Human Resources who are career-minded and success oriented, but much too busy to read those same old boring HR books.*

# START HERE

## TWO WARNINGS BEFORE YOU READ ON

This story addresses one of the biggest frustrations that you'll ever face in your career in HR. And that's getting passed over for that promotion that you worked hard for and thought you richly deserved.

Personally, I've been in this boat five times in my twenty-five year HR career. If you've ever experienced this yourself, you know how devastating it can be. Whether you truly believed you deserved the job or were promised it by your boss or the higher ups, no one likes being denied that next move up the ladder of success. It can keep you up at night for weeks struggling to figure out what went wrong.

However, this isn't a unique situation.

**Just about everyone in HR gets rejected for a job at some point in their career.**

And the story you're about to read will take you into the world of Drake Williams, an HR director who gets passed over for a promotion...and absolutely does NOT see it coming...and loses this job to a person that shocks him beyond belief. And yes, it's a heart wrenching experience for him too. But what will he do about it? What lessons will he learn in the process? How does all this apply to you? Well, I guess you'll have to dive into these pages to find out.

**One hint: The powerful secret he learned about advancing his career is revealed at the very end of this book.** And it's a secret you can apply in your own career to minimize your chances of getting overlooked for future promotions...whether they arise within or outside of your current organization.

Frankly, I wish I would have known about this secret years ago when I first started in HR. It would have saved me lots of pain and agony. Nevertheless, I believe if you embrace it now, it will create a massive breakthrough in your HR career.

With all that said, here are two warnings:

**WARNING #1: Do NOT skip ahead to the end to discover what this secret is.** Doing so will only diminish its impact. It will be revealed soon enough, so take your time to enjoy this engaging story first. I assure you it will be worth the wait. This book is a quick read and written so that you will fully appreciate the "golden lesson" waiting for you at the end.

**WARNING #2: This is a FICTIONAL STORY and is not based on anyone's actual experience.** All the names, characters, organizations, products or events are imaginary and are used fictitiously. You should also know that this book is FOR ADULTS ONLY. That means you'll encounter profanity and mature adult situations, much like what you'll find in the business world. If you are not offended watching PG-18 or R-rated movies on cable TV, then this story should not offend you either. That said, I can't guarantee that you won't be stunned or taken aback at times. But consider that all part of the journey.

**Last but certainly not least, I want to give a huge shout out to Allison Quinn, my co-author, for agreeing to help me write this book!** She is an awesomely gifted, up and coming novelist and fiction writer, who has a knack for creating relatable characters and intriguing stories. While I provided the plot and HR insights, this book would not have been possible without Allison's prodigious story-telling talent to bring all of this to life.

You're about the fall into one of her roller-coaster tales that will grip you right from start to finish. So buckle up, dive in and enjoy the ride!

Best Regards,
*Alan Collins*

# 1

## THE HIDDEN SPOT

"Damn! You scared the hell out of me. I thought you were a wild animal."

"Sorry, lady, I didn't mean to startle you. And take it from me, you ain't gonna find no wild animals here...unless you're talking about muggers."

"Muggers! How do you know so much about muggers?"

"Grew up with 'em. Some of 'em were my best friends."

AND WITH THAT SUDDEN, TOTALLY UNEXPECTED ENCOUNTER, Drake Williams and Clare Hammond met for the first time.

In this hidden spot right by Lake Michigan.

In Chicago.

The world famous Windy City.

Drake jogged to this little-known spot by the lake from his nearby downtown condo every day at 5 o'clock in the morning. This particular place was concealed by a tall row of pine trees that always made his run smell like Christmas, even in the dead of summer. Not surprisingly, he didn't run into many people when he got there.

But, on this particular day, he found this unfamiliar woman there. Someone who clearly wasn't expecting to see him.

And she was sitting on "his" tree stump.

This very small stump could only seat one person at a time. And, after his run, he'd sit there and meditate every morning.

UNFORTUNATELY, HE COULDN'T TODAY.

This unwelcomed intruder had parked her butt on his spot.

So Drake positioned himself a few feet away from her and decided to do his meditation and some stretching exercises standing up. However, as he flexed his body, he couldn't help but shoot occasional glances in her direction. She was stunningly gorgeous despite wearing a dull, baggy jogging outfit. Her blonde hair fell to just past her shoulders and her blue eyes looked like the pure lake water just a few yards away. Her lips were bright red, thick and full and he couldn't believe she had lipstick on so early in the morning. It was all kind of irresistible and frankly just a little distracting.

After a few minutes of continuing to sneak quick peeks her way, he thought he might as well introduce himself. After all, it was the polite thing to do.

"Hi, I'm Drake. You come here often? I thought I'd be alone here this morning."

"No, I don't. This is actually my first visit to Chicago. I'm Clare, by the way. Whenever I come to a city for the first time, I typically go for an early morning run to just explore. I thought I'd rest here on this stump. A college friend of mine told me about this special place. And she was right. I have to say that this view of Lake Michigan through the trees is just breathtaking. Is it one of your favorite places to stop?"

"Yep, it is. And I…"

SUDDENLY DRAKE FELT HIS CELL PHONE buzz in the pocket of his shorts.

"Excuse me…"

Looking down at his phone, he saw an urgent text message from his boss. Damn! He was going to need to cut this conversation short.

Meanwhile, Clare kept chatting away, oblivious to it all.

"Have you ever gone swimming in that lake? It's so beautiful. When I was a little girl, my uncle thought it would be easy to teach me to swim, by throwing me in the nearby lake just like this one. His dad had done it to him, and he'd learned pretty quickly. But for me, it took awhile. The first time, I was so scared that I froze, and when I started sinking, he had to dive in to save me. Eventually, though, it worked. And that's how I learned how to swim. Do you swim?"

"NOPE!"

He hoped his curt and abrupt response would send the subtle message to leave him alone so he could quickly finish up his morning meditation so he could get going.

Not a chance.

She ignored him and just kept talking.

He thought, why won't this woman just shut the hell up? He was now pissed off that he had even spoken to her in the first place. He didn't even know her and here she was running off at the mouth nonstop, preventing him from squeezing in his final moments of silent meditation.

Maybe at a different time, he'd chat her up too, given that she was so attractive. In fact, years ago, when he was active on the dating scene, he'd hit her up for her number and attempt to hook up with her later. But not these days. Besides he didn't have that kind of time right now. And so he finished his exercises, then abruptly said: "Hey, gotta go!" and with that he then took off to finish up his morning run.

As he jogged away, he couldn't resist. He took one last quick, curious peek back over his shoulder towards at her.

She was staring at him.

He turned his head forward and smiled in admiration.

HE THEN SHIFTED HIS MIND TO A MORE PRESSING PRIORITY...namely that urgent text message he just got.

# 2

# DRAKE

Drake Williams is Director of Human Resources at the headquarters of the NuStyle Foods & Snacks Corporation – or Nu Foods, as it's referred to by everyone.

Nu Foods is a mid-sized, global organization specializing in innovative breakfast products, snack foods and healthy drinks. Five years ago they moved their corporate headquarters from the suburbs to downtown Chicago. They were following the lead of lots of companies that were relocating back to the city after decades away. And there were many reasons why.

The booming downtown and thriving business community.

World class restaurants, shopping and entertainment.

Brand new start-ups and expanding technology resources.

Stunning, million-dollar condos in the city with awesome views.

AND THE AVAILABILITY OF WORLD CLASS TALENT as well. Executives, millennials and talented people from around the globe were being drawn in droves to the Chicago downtown neighborhoods and the growing number of six-figure jobs at the many Fortune 1000 companies nearby.

All of these factors attracted Drake here too.

He purchased his downtown condo right by Lake Michigan three years ago before all the real estate prices got insane. He loves his place, even though he rarely takes time to enjoy it.

HIS LIFE TODAY IS QUITE A CONTRAST with how he grew up. He was raised in a tough, all-black neighborhood five hours away in Detroit. As a kid, he could remember both his parents coming home exhausted. His mom from teaching science classes at Cooley High School. His father from working as a mechanic on the graveyard shift at the local General Motors factory. In particular, he remembers his dad always smelling like oil and gasoline, which no doubt came from toiling away on the assembly line repairing car engines.

Both parents worked hard.

They never missed a day on their jobs. Both retired on the same day and celebrated with a big retirement party that folks in Detroit still talk about. For the last few years, they have been living in Sarasota, Florida, relocating to a small home in a retirement community after they sacrificed, and saved up for over thirty years to finally buy it. They were now living their dream.

They wanted the same thing for Drake, their only child. And growing up they stressed the work ethic. Constantly.

"NOBODY'S GONNA GIVE BLACK FOLKS SHIT!" he remembers his dad telling him. "You gotta willing to bust your ass. That's the key to making it in this goddamn life. Hard ass work."

His mom would chime in and pile on: "Son, listen to your dad, he's right. You can't count on white folks handing you anything. You're going to have to earn it. And you're going to need a good education too."

He can still hear these words ringing in his ears, constantly, nonstop after all these years.

But he's learned their lessons well.

He graduated cum laude in Business from University of Michigan and picked up his HR certification later from the Society of Human Resource Management (SHRM). And, in their minds, he is now a big shot at a huge corporation and has far exceeded their wildest expectations. Their only wish for him now is to settle down and give them some grandkids.

However, Drake has different priorities. He isn't going to rest until he reaches the top HR job -- Vice President of Human Resources at Nu Foods. Nothing else is more important. He is obsessed. Becoming the most senior executive in HR there would be a crowning achievement, making him the highest ranking African-African at the company. He believes it will make his hardworking parents even prouder and will be a source of pride for him as well.

TO MAKE THIS HAPPEN, for the last couple of years he's taken his long ingrained work ethic to the extreme. It has now become all-consuming obsession. He's a workaholic with zero personal life to speak of. He stopped dating two years ago to eliminate "distractions." He's ignored his college classmates and his buddies from the old neighborhood who, in frustration, have stopped calling him when they visit the city. And he's all but eliminated networking and going to the local SHRM Association meetings because he is just too exhausted at the end of the day.

He just keeps his head down.

Grinding away at his day job.

Going in early.

Staying late.

Remaining focused on his ONE goal – earning that promotion into that HR VP position. And dismissing anyone and anything not related to achieving it.

Just like his parents taught him back in Detroit.

And he has gotten even more excited about his chances in the last few weeks, because he's heard through the grapevine that the current occupant in that job, his boss Lois, is going to retire. If that happens, based on his hard work and great performance, he has no doubt that he'll be tapped to replace her.

Those were the things that were rolling around in his mind while this Clare woman was chatting away by the lake at his private spot…and when he got that urgent text message.

THAT TEXT WAS FROM LOIS.

Maybe…just maybe, it was news about her retirement.

And his promotion.

# 3

## THE CALL TO LIZ

For some strange reason, Clare Hammond's mind kept drifting back to that stunning hidden spot on the lake…and to that Drake dude. She couldn't shake the image of him flexing and doing his exercises right in front of her.

And she couldn't understand why.

Sure he had a great body, but there was something else.

Something a little different about him.

The only way to handle such a problem was Liz. Liz was her college roommate years ago and still her best friend. Picking up her phone, she got Liz on the line.

"Hello."

"Hey, Liz. It's Clare." There was a slight pause on the other end of the line, then an excited voice filtered through the phone.

"HEY! HOW ARE THINGS GOING UP IN CHICAGO? DID YOU GET MUGGED YET? Did you see anyone get murdered? I've been keeping up with the news every day just so I can make sure that you're not on a slab somewhere."

Clare didn't know whether to thank her friend, or feel creeped out by her.

"Thanks, I think. Things are fine. I'm staying here at the Sheraton just off of North Michigan Avenue. And I just went for a run this morning along the lake. I think I'm going to stay for a few more days here just to check things out. I just love this city. But hey, I ran into this really hot dude who looked like a young Denzel Washington.

"Anyway, Liz, he's about six feet two, with a tight ass and built like a body builder. He didn't say much to me, but when he spoke he had this sexy baritone voice. I can't get him out of my mind."

"Oooh! A black guy who looked like Denzel. Wow! I bet you really wanted to hop on that, huh? Did you check out the size of his feet? You know what they say."

Clare blushed. That was one of the things about Liz. She was so brazen and blunt that she hardly ever knew when she was embarrassing someone. Thankfully this was a phone call, and she couldn't see Clare turn beet red.

"He was a little snooty, actually. I think he resented me being in his little spot. It almost felt like he owned the place and was being protective of it. I don't know what the hell was up with him. But, he didn't seem to want to talk to me at all. I know I shouldn't care. But I'm confused. What did I do wrong?"

"Clare, you know those big city guys can be real assholes. My advice, forget him. You got too much to offer and he sounds like an arrogant prick to me. There's no way he's in your league. I know you're horny and you want to laid, but get your mind back on why you're there, girl. Go dazzle those big city folks and go get that job and that money."

The two friends laughed and talked back and forth for the better part of a half hour before Clare finally hung up the phone.

She was smiling.

She missed Liz, but even from a distance she could work her magic and cheer her up no matter what the case was.

Once she didn't have the distraction of Liz to occupy her time anymore, she found her thoughts floating back to Drake. She hadn't dated anyone in six months and hated to admit it, Liz was right, she needed to get laid. Maybe that was it. Anyway, she had to admit that she wouldn't mind seeing him again…even if it was only for that sexy body of his.

Thinking about him, reminded her of something that Liz had jokingly said, and it bothered her. Liz had told her to be careful because she might end up staying in Chicago for the men and not the job. She tried to laugh it off, but in all honesty, she could see it happening if she wasn't careful.

But besides Drake, she did have more important things on her mind.

SHE THEN GLANCED AT A FOLDED PIECE OF PAPER that was lying on the nightstand near her bed. That piece of paper was the whole reason that she was in Chicago in the first place. She went over, unfolded it and began to scan the letter over again. It was three pages, single-spaced, describing the details of her important interview that would be a major step up in her career.

After looking up from the letter, she set it aside with a sigh and picked up her phone. She then checked her emails to make sure that nothing too terrible was happening back on the job in Kansas City.

Once she'd gotten through everything, promptly deleting all of the junk emails, she put down her phone.

Again, she couldn't help thinking about that guy she'd met that morning.

# 4

## CLARE

Clare Hammond is thirty-five years old and excited about her upcoming interview.

She currently works at the Allaco Beverage Company, a global manufacturer of private-label healthy drinks based in Kansas City. She loves her job there, but has gotten passed over for a promotion for the second time in six months. After getting no clear feedback or support from her self-centered boss, she isn't about to stay there and let it happen again. She's hopeful that a new job opportunity set up by her executive recruiter friend in Chicago will prove fruitful.

Her best bud Liz is absolutely right, Clare indeed has a lot to offer.

HER RESUME would impress just about any organization. She got her Bachelor's and Master's degrees at University of Illinois in five years and captained the Big Ten championship swim team while there.

If that wasn't enough, she was also voted Miss Illinois second runner up. She is clearly physically attractive, and people often tell her she's is a dead ringer for the singer, Carrie Underwood – a resemblance that has been both alluring and distracting to the guys she's worked with.

Despite this, she rarely flaunts her looks. In fact, she is a little self-conscious when people glance at her more than a few seconds because she had bad acne growing up and believes it is still visible. It isn't, but it still makes her a bit insecure when people stare.

And while she's not overly flirtatious, she does have a sixth sense and can tell when the guys who work around her are scoping her out...and she could tell that Drake was looking her over earlier that morning, even though he tried to hide it.

PEOPLE INSTINCTIVELY GRAVITATE TO HER also because she is warm, upbeat and outgoing. However, underneath her extroverted, chatty façade is a driven woman, hugely ambitious who believes in aggressively managing her career and going after the things she wants.

In fact, a sentence from one of her many job reference letters sums her up perfectly: "If you want a real go getter, a real leader who gets along great with everyone, but who can be tough as nails and get things done, Clare Hammond is who you want."

Nevertheless, she has been clawing her way up the corporate ladder for the last ten years and her personal life is far from textbook perfect.

She never met her dad and was raised by an alcoholic single mom. They both lived in and out of various basements and trailer parks. They even spent a week living in an abandoned car for awhile, when her mom lost her job. All these rough experiences, and her mom's suicide at age 45, have all steeled her resolve and motivated her to pursue her dreams even more. She compensates for her rough upbringing by presenting a strong, invincible front to those around her, appearing confident in just about every situation. But on the inside, she still clings onto the insecurities that shaped her childhood years.

Despite all her struggles growing up, she always thrived academically, athletically and socially from high school on. She got into Illinois on a swimming scholarship and along the way has built a great circle of relationships. Everyone loves Clare because she loves them back and enjoys having a good time. "Work hard, play hard" is her mantra.

Every couple of years she taps into her vast personal network of college and business contacts to help her change jobs to get ahead. After working in three different companies, she's now looking to settle down in one place for the long haul.

And there is another reason she's seeking some stability.

FOUR YEARS AGO, she married a guy she thought was perfect.

Unfortunately, they wed before really getting a chance to know each other, and it didn't work out. When he lost his job, he got lazy, started gambling and just wanted to spend her money as fast as she could make it. And that wasn't going to work with Clare. One day, when she refused give him five hundred bucks, he slapped her in the face. She then kicked him in the nuts and called the police. That was it. His butt had to go. It has been two years since their divorce was finalized. It was extremely painful at first and she avoided dating for a year. But now she has finally and emotionally put this bad episode behind her and is open to exploring a serious relationship again.

However, this time will be different.

After her divorce, she had a long conversation with a marriage counselor, one of her many career mentors, who suggested she develop a list of *guiding principles* and a mental checklist that she follow for her next serious romantic relationship.

And she has.

She wants to find someone who has the stability that her ex-husband lacked, as well as a whole slew of other things too.

That's why she couldn't get that Drake guy out of her head. He clearly met some of the items on her checklist. And he was hot, handsome and professional in a quiet sort of way.

Yes, their conversation was very brief.

But there was something mysterious and deeply intriguing about him.

# 5

## THE MEETING WITH LOIS

"Hey, hold that elevator, Boris!"

"Thanks. These elevators are so darn slow and I didn't want to be late for my meeting."

"I know what you mean. What's up, Drake?"

"EARLY MORNING MEETING WITH THE BOSS. And I don't want to keep her waiting."

With that, Drake got in and rode up to the 25th floor. During the ride, he was trying to keep his mind off that sexy woman that had intruded on his secret little corner of the world by the lake.

The only woman he wanted to focus on right now was Lois Wellington.

Lois is Drake's boss and the current Vice President of Human Resources. She's fifty-five years old, has been with Nu Foods for twenty-five years and was the first female senior executive at the company. Having been in that top HR job for over ten years, she knows everything and everybody.

She has short gray hair, and ice blue eyes that flash like chips of pure lightning when she's angry. Drake has often said she reminds him of Judi Dench, the British actress who played James Bond's boss in the movies. Because like Dench, she is a strong, perceptive and commanding woman, who takes no bullshit from anyone. And because of this, she's highly respected by everyone and a force within the organization.

LOIS KNOWS THE BUSINESS COLD and is off-the-charts brilliant about HR. And she's progressed rapidly within the company because of it.

However, at times, she can be extremely withdrawn and standoffish. She really doesn't open up to a lot of people, isn't big on team meetings and lots of personal interaction – preferring instead email, texts and brief five-minute updates with her team.

But when she gets pissed off, which is surprisingly often, she pulls no punches. She's blunt and can curse up a storm. And there's a long list of people in the organization who have experienced this brutally profane side of Lois' personality...and it's something few want to repeat.

Despite all this, Drake has built a great relationship with her. However, not by creating lots of warm and fuzzy interactions, because she isn't that type of boss. Instead he quietly supports her agenda, works like a dog to take projects off her plate and does the little noticeable things to make himself look good in her eyes – while trying not to be an obvious suck up, ass kisser and in her face all the time.

IN RETURN, SHE ALWAYS MAKES TIME for coaching, advice or to share her prodigious intellect with him. So he is pleased when she scheduled this early morning "confidential" meeting.

If the rumors about her retiring are true, this could be an important conversation. When he reached Floor 25, Lois surprisingly was right there to greet him at the elevator. After some brief small talk, they walked to her office and then she closed her door behind them. He was hoping this was going to be the big day and so he did his best to tamp down his excitement.

"Drake, glad you got my text and thanks for coming in extra early. Let me get right to the point."

So far, so good. This might be going his way if he played his cards right. He sat up straight, giving his professionalism a definite boost, just in case.

"Yesterday, I talked to Grisham and told him I had made up my mind and that I plan to step down and retire early. Grisham, as the CEO of this company, rightfully needed to know my decision first. Together, we decided I'd hang around a month or so to help onboard the new person and wrap up a few confidential things before heading out for the final time."

"Drake, now that I'm fifty-five, it's time. I love HR and I'll probably do some consulting or Board work later on. But right now I'm all burnt out. I'm tired of all the travel I have to do to deal with all of the union and labor issues in our factories. And I also need a permanent break from all the politics and sexist bullshit I've had to put up with being the most senior woman in this organization.

"I've been financially secure for some time now. And I'm ready to spend the rest of my life with Thomas, doing the things that old married folks like us should be doing, while we still can. While this place can be a pain in the ass, I've really loved working here. But, it's time to go. I'm ready to start a new chapter of my life, and--"

At that point Drake interrupted, so excited he couldn't restrain himself.

"Lois, thank you for sharing that. To be honest, I didn't know if the rumors were true about you retiring. And since you didn't say anything, I didn't want to bring it up. But now that I know, you should know that a lot of people around here are going to miss you. I, for one, owe you my whole career. You've been a phenomenal mentor and boss. Thomas is a lucky guy and I know you guys will enjoy yourselves in retirement. And--"

"Drake, you're kind," Lois said cutting him off, "but let me finish. My retirement is the just the first part of what I wanted to talk to you about. There is a second part. And it relates to you."

Uh oh, here it comes.

"I know you've worked hard. You know how I feel about what you've accomplished. But...as much as I'd like to tell you something different…I can't guarantee that you will be the one that gets my job. Grisham wants the best person. So he and the leadership team are going to bring in an outside candidate to interview too. Everybody knows who you are and what you can do. But they also want to know what's in the external marketplace as well, so they can do a comparison before making their final choice."

"Now don't get me wrong. I've been lobbying like hell for you behind the scenes with him and the leadership team. And, of course, Grisham's going to make the final choice. But make no mistake about this, he knows how I feel. I've told him that you're hands down, the top candidate for my job. Your work, especially leading the effort to update our talent management programs and HR technology has been outstanding and highly valued by everybody."

"Thanks Lois. I appreciate that."

"And one other thing, Drake…for me, personally, I can't thank you enough for helping me with my presentations to Grisham and the Board. You know how much I hate that dog and pony shit. The work you do for us makes you a goddamn superstar in my mind. But hell, I'm only one voice and I'm biased. And, in the end, it's his decision. And the senior leadership team's. They're going to have to live with the person replacing me."

She went on to describe what Grisham was looking for in her successor. As he heard more, Drake had no doubt he met all of the CEO's criteria.

"I appreciate your support and your brutal honesty as always, Lois. You always shoot straight with me. That means a lot. I understand they're gonna pick the best person for the job. It's no different than what we do in HR when we're filling any other job here. So it all makes sense. I just know I've been working my butt off doing everything I can to make sure that I meet the criteria for this job. And I'm thrilled you've told Grisham and the rest of the higher ups that."

Lois smiled at him, very much like a proud mother.

"I know you do Drake. It'll take a week or so to finish up that other candidate's interview. Hey, one good thing, I almost forgot. I asked them to interview you last. That should give you the advantage of being the person that's the most fresh in all their minds. I haven't seen that other candidate yet, but it goes without saying that you're my number one choice."

DRAKE WAS ELATED WHEN HE HEARD THAT.

He knew that there was no one else in the company that had influence and clout like Lois. And he also knew there was no one else half as qualified for Lois' job as he was.

However, he did wonder how long it would take for them to make the final decision after the interviews were done. After all, the new person would need to spend some time with Lois, before she left, to fully get up to speed.

So he hoped it would happen soon.

And it would.

# 6

## ON THE STUMP AGAIN

The next day Clare went to that stump by the lake again. She wanted to get her morning run in.

And while she didn't want to admit to herself, she was also hoping that she'd run into that hunky Drake guy again. She'd been thinking about him ever since she'd gotten off the phone with Liz.

Unlike the baggy outfit she had on yesterday, she dressed differently today.

Tight black yoga pants.

Florescent green running shoes.

Sports watch.

Her lucky bright red lipstick.

And one more thing, a black low-cut, V-necked tank top that would set off her best assets.

Just in case Drake was going to make his morning run to the spot again, she'd wanted to look her best. So she set out on her one-mile jog from the hotel at the crack of dawn, not knowing exactly if or when he was going to be there. But guessing from the last time, she felt she might not be waiting for very long.

AS WAS USUALLY THE CASE, SHE WAS RIGHT.

She'd barely arrived and sat down on the stump, looking out over the lake, when she heard the rustling of the bushes behind her.

She took a deep breath and turned around to face the intruder.

Her heart skipped half a beat when she saw that it was indeed Drake.

She offered him a smile, and saw that he was a little surprised to see her. But there was a different, brighter sparkle in his eyes today, something that she couldn't quite make out enough to get a clear reading on.

"Good morning. Don't tell me you come here every day?" She teased.

She'd remembered he'd said "yes" when she'd asked him before if he came here often, but to her "often" and "every day" were two completely different things.

"As a matter of fact, I DO. I'm here every day. And this morning is beautiful. But wait, before you say anything else...let me apologize for yesterday. I realized that I was just a bit rude to you when I ran off. You were just trying to be polite to me."

Her eyes widened as she noticed that he'd actually said more than a couple of sentences instead of one word answers. He was clearly in a more positive and upbeat mood today.

"Hey, apology not needed. My bad. I was just being me. My BFF, Liz thinks that I talk too much anyway and that I have no filters whatsoever when it comes to meeting new people and chatting them up. That's why she won't go to the bar with me anymore."

Drake smiled at her, as he bent down to touch his toes, then stood up as straight as he could before twisting his upper body to the left and right. Between these exercise moves, he could see she had cute dimples on her cheeks that he hadn't noticed the day before.

"So I take it that the bar scene isn't really your thing then?"

Caught by surprise at his assumption, Clare laughed.

"Oh, bars are cool! I love 'em. I just have to go by myself now because no one wants to go with me there anymore. But I really like restaurants that have a dance floor, or even a night club or two so I can unleash some energy through my horrible dancing." She clapped her hand over her mouth quickly, realizing that she'd shared too much personal information. He laughed at her good naturedly, and she saw that his eyes sparkled again, almost like light flashing.

"So, what do you think of this place?" he said. She was grateful to him for changing the subject to something a lot less capable of making her say something to embarrass herself again.

"It's magical. That's the main reason I came back here," she exaggerated, as it was only half of the real reason.

"If you think this place is great, you should go to Navy Pier. Have you been there yet? The view of the Chicago skyline from there is beautiful at night. In fact, on a clear day, from there you can see three different states -- Wisconsin, Indiana and Michigan. It's amazing. And if you ever get a chance, go to the top of Hancock building, the view of the city from there is awesome too."

"I haven't been to either of those places yet, but I've caught glimpses of night skyline from my hotel room. You're right. I know it's brutal here in the wintertime, but this city is sooo beautiful in the summer. I just don't see these kinds of views at all back in Kansas City. I'm torn, really. I don't know what's more stunning -- the skyline or this lake. But, I'm a swimmer and so I have a soft spot in my heart for anything aquatic."

"Boy, I wish I learned to swim. But I didn't. Hey, since you're from out of town, how much do you know about Chicago's history?"

"Nothing, really. All I remember reading somewhere is that back in the day, Al Capone and his gangsters ravaged the town, but I couldn't tell you much more beyond that."

"Hey, no problem. Let me clue you in on some great things about Chicago most folks don't know about...."

He grinned and began describing some of his favorite places in the city. The more he talked, the more she was mesmerized by his articulateness, his deep voice, his mannerisms and most of all, that chiseled body that he had. She could see a little more of it now than she could the day before because today he had on spandex shorts and a tight muscle shirt on for his morning exercises.

As she nodded and smiled, he seemed to get more comfortable and forgot all about his workout. He sat on the ground in front of her, while she remained seated on "his" stump.

THEY LAUGHED AND TALKED FOR OVER AN HOUR.

During their conversation, he got so relaxed and unguarded that he took a deep breath and launched into the story of his potential promotion and what had happened to him in Lois' office the day before. It didn't seem to matter that she was just some stranger he'd just met. She was a fantastic listener and so easy to talk to. She gave him her undivided attention, nodded and smiled at all the right times.

When he finished, she congratulated him and wished him good luck. "To be honest, I'm in town for a job interview myself and I'm very excited about it too."

"Hey, I'm sure that you'll get that job. You strike me as a very bright woman and somebody who knows what to do to get what she wants."

She smiled, knowing that her cheeks were probably a brilliant shade of red right now.

"Thank you. What a nice thing to say. I do hope I can nail my interview. After all, it would be a horrible waste for me to come here all the way from Kansas City and not get offered the job. I don't handle rejection too well, and I might not be so friendly to the people that called me out here if they wanted to hire someone else."

She paused, then fiddled with her sports watch for a second or two before she took a deep breath and decided to take a risk – a big risk. "Hey, I was thinking, if you don't have any other plans, perhaps we could go out for a drink tonight after you get off work, and you can tell me more about this city. I'd love to know more about it, especially if I wind up getting a job here."

There, she said it. The ball was now in his court.

His smile disappeared and he stared at her for what seemed like an eternity. And when she was just about to ask if there was something on her face, he got up and turned away from her abruptly. Then looking at his watch, said: "Can't! I'm late. Really gotta go!"

And then, without warning, he ran off.

Clare was shocked to say the least.

THIS WAS THE SECOND DAMN TIME.

What a fucking asshole!

Why would he be so nice and polite and then leave so rudely?

Hey, what about giving me an explanation about why you're leaving, Drake?

Hey, what about going out another night, if tonight doesn't work, Drake?

Hey, what's with you, Drake?

Confused. It didn't make sense to her.

Sure, it wasn't the first time that she'd been turned down, but she thought he might have a little more sensitivity, especially since she'd just told him that she didn't deal too well with rejection. Apparently, that part of the conversation had just gone over his head.

She decided that she'd simply just shrug it off and not let it bother her.

Besides her job interview was later today, and she wasn't going to let one jerk in the whole city of Chicago ruin her day. She was more resilient than that, and besides she knew that she could pick up a guy at any bar in town, if she wanted to.

Although she'd never, ever, ever do that.

Anyway, she quickly got her mind off him as she arrived back at her room.

Once there, she showered and began getting ready.

She wanted no drama or delays in getting to her interview. So she had the hotel concierge schedule an experienced limo driver to pick her up. That way she could quietly collect herself along the way and be assured of arriving ten minutes early.

She then pulled out her power outfit -- a dark skirt with the matching jacket along with a light lavender, button down blouse. After sliding on a pair of black pumps, she brushed her blonde hair until it shone.

And with a light dusting of makeup, she was ready.

# 7

## OFFICE BUZZ

Drake felt like a complete jackass but he had to get the hell out of there.

This woman had just casually asked him out on a date and he was nowhere near ready for a time-consuming, intimate relationship.

He knew from experience that it took guts for a woman to put herself out there like she did. But his walls came up and he bailed like a frightened little six-year old boy afraid of girls.

This beautiful woman, Clare, could be a major distraction to him. And right now, he didn't need distractions.

He was too close.

He just about had his dream job in hand.

But he was confused. He'd gone to the spot as he did every day and deep down was hoping to see her there as well. He would never have admitted that last fact to himself, but he knew it was true. He had wanted to apologize for the complete and utter jackass he had been the first time that they'd met.

And he'd done that.

They'd talked for a long time and everything seemed to be going fine.

He really enjoyed being with her. And he could tell she liked him too, otherwise she wouldn't have asked him out for drinks after work.

It was probably worth the risk, but for some unfathomable reason, he got scared and bailed.

And, on top of all this, he remembered that mere minutes before, she mentioned that she really didn't do well with rejection. And now he'd rejected her and didn't even have the guts to tell her the real reason why.

His face fell with regret and shame.

After a few horribly mournful minutes completely lost in thought, he broke his trance and glanced at his watch.

"Fuck!" he muttered. He'd spent too long thinking about her.

Now he REALLY needed to get to work.

Once he got home, he hurled himself into the shower and then threw on his clothes. Part of him didn't even care if he went into the office or not, and that was his first clue that there was something wrong. He never, ever missed a day of work, no matter what.

Thinking back, he remembered one close call. It happened on a day where he and Lois had a big presentation to the Board on the new human resources strategy. He had come down with the flu, felt terrible and thought about calling Lois to tell her he wasn't going to make it. But he didn't want to let her down. So, at the last minute, he dragged himself out of bed, hopped a taxi and rushed into the Board Meeting with about a minute to spare.

The same thing happened on this day. He rushed in at about 8:30 a.m. which was late for him. Naturally, just about everyone was there already, which was no surprise.

However, something seemed strange.

As he took the long walk to his office, other employees looked up at him from behind their cubicle walls and began to whisper and snicker. This was highly unusual and he wasn't at all sure that he liked it.

He made his way to his desk, walking slowly while straining his ears to try to catch a few phrases of the whispered conversations that were going on around him. He caught an occasional word or two, but it wasn't enough to nail down what the buzz was all about. He decided that he would find out sooner or later, if it was really important.

As he sat down and booted up his laptop, a shadow fell across his desk, and he turned around to see who it was.

"Hey, mornin' Drake. What's up, dude?" It was Mike Tanner, the Total Rewards Director, a peer of his who was a royal pain in the ass and the biggest gossip in the company. Drake forced a smile. There was no way in hell he wanted to sit here for an hour making small talk about who was screwing who in the office or debating local politics with a guy that just loved to hear himself talk. Now was not the time.

But he was curious about what was happening.

"Morning, Mike. I'm fine. Hey, looks like something's going on in the office. Did I miss some news?"

"Well, everybody's buzzing about the rumor."

"What rumor is that?"

"The rumor that you might not be getting Lois' VP gig after all," he said pausing to let his words sink in.

RIGHT AWAY, DRAKE GOT A HORRIBLE FEELING in the pit of his stomach. No, that couldn't be true. Lois was firmly in his corner.

"Bullshit! No way. And just how the hell do you know that, Mr. Goddamn Know-it-All?"

"Well...I don't really know that for sure," Mike admitted. "I just know that they flew someone in today to interview for Lois' job. I thought I'd give you a heads up. But the way you're snapping at me tells me that maybe I should have just left you alone. See you later, dude!"

And with that, Mike turned around in a huff and walked away, leaving Drake with his mouth open.

Drake wanted to explain that he knew all about the interview from Lois and to remind him that it was always the HR policy to interview at least one person from the outside for senior positions, but Mike didn't give him a chance.

Ignoring the office chatter and whispers that were flying all around him, Drake went back to his laptop to catch up on his emails. When bad things happened, as usual, he threw himself into his work.

However, he couldn't help daydreaming about how good it felt to talk to Clare at the stump a few hours ago. The more he thought about their conversation, the more he wished that he could let his hair down and talk to someone like her all the time. With no real close buddy, mentor or career sounding board, he missed having someone to confide in about his job, the challenges he faced and his career ambitions. She was a great listener, empathized and didn't interrupt like most people. In fact, it seemed like she actually understood his job and what he did. If he could have someone like her, anyone, maybe he wouldn't feel so alone.

He sighed.

Then he got up to refill his coffee cup in the HR break room. And in the process, he could feel every eye in the place again shooting glances at him with the whispering reaching a level that he couldn't ignore. It seemed like the people around him were enjoying the fact that he might not get the top HR job.

That pissed him off.

As he poured his cup, his hands were tightening into fists and he risked crushing the paper cup that held his decaf. Unnerved, he decided to go down to the cafeteria to drink his coffee and perhaps grab a bagel.

At least down there, there were fewer people he'd know. When he arrived, he sat by himself at a corner table with his snack.

He thought about how he could actually use a drink or two after work. And he was suddenly regretting the fact that he'd run out on Clare. He was thinking that it would be nice to sit at a bar with her and tell her about the awful day he'd had, while they sipped something a little stronger than just coffee.

Oh well...

# 8

## THE BOARD ROOM INTERVIEW

Clare got into her scheduled limo outside of the hotel and confirmed the address of the interview with the driver.

She was nervous, but ready.

She spent the entire ride going over in her mind, for seemingly the hundredth time, all the potential questions the interviewers
might throw at her and how she'd respond.

She had the letter that the company had emailed to her in her
purse. And she kept her hand on it until the driver dropped her
off, almost as if she was afraid that it might magically disappear.
She had read it over at least fifty times. But because of her
nerves, she had trouble remembering all the details it contained.
For example, the floor and the office number, and the name of
the person that was going to be interviewing her. She didn't
want to screw this up. This was a fantastic opportunity and she
was ready to do just about anything to get it.

Even though it was now crunch time, every now and then her
mind would float back to Drake. And the weird encounter they'd
had earlier that morning. He had apologized for his rude behavior the previous day, and they'd sat there and talked for what
seemed like an eternity. Everything was going fine until she'd
asked him out for drinks. She was beating herself up for that

now, not knowing if that was the reason that made him turn tail and run.

She sighed.

No time to worry about all that now.

IT WAS TIME TO GO UPSTAIRS FOR HER INTERVIEW.

This was the moment of truth. She had to be on her game. Taking a deep breath, she took the letter out of her purse to read it again one more time. Confirming the floor and the office, she got in the elevator and pushed the button.

The whole way up she repeated the woman's name over and over again in her head so her nerves wouldn't let her forget. "Lois... Lois... Lois..."

When the elevator doors opened, a woman about her own age was standing behind a receptionist desk in front of a wall displaying the large Nu Foods company logo. This woman was talking on the phone and wearing an expensive Louis Vuitton outfit. In comparison, Clare felt frumpy and plain in her outfit that probably cost half as much. And it was almost enough to make her turn tail and run back out of there.

But she wasn't going to do that.

This was her chance.

THIS WAS THE OPPORTUNITY THAT SHE'D BEEN LOOKING FOR. This was the job that was potentially going to set the trajectory for the rest of her career. If she landed it, her career would reach a new high point. No, she wasn't going to leave no matter how nervous she was. Then she remembered, this is the way she felt at the Big Ten Swimming Championships when she was in college. She was nervous then too, but she walked away with two gold medals. No reason to think that can't happen now too, she thought.

So she squared her shoulders under her dark business suit jacket and walked towards the woman behind the desk with what she hoped was a confident gait. As she got closer, this receptionist wasn't nearly as intimidating as she appeared. Clare had thought that she'd have to stand in front of her and clear her throat loudly to get her attention. But no, the woman immediately looked up at her with a smile before she even made it up to the desk.

"Good morning and welcome to Nu Foods. Can I help you?"

Wow, she's much more polite than she appeared. Maybe this wouldn't turn out to be such a bad day after all.

"Good morning. I'm here to see Lois Wellington for an interview. It's for the HR VP position." There, she'd remembered the name and she'd even managed to smile back at the woman.

"Great. You must be Clare Hammond. If you'll follow me, I'll take you to the Board Room. It won't just be Lois that you're meeting with, but also the senior leadership team and Grisham Perry, our CEO as well."

Clare froze in her tracks for just a second or two.

Damn. No one told her that this was going to be a group interview. She'd thought she'd be meeting individually with just Lois, the CEO and two other executives mentioned in her letter.

Separately. Not all together.

THEY'D JUST THROWN HER A DAMN CURVE BALL.

Was this a test?

If so, she didn't like it.

This just added to her nervousness. She took a few rapid breaths just to try to get her nerves settled down.

But it didn't work.

Now a lot less confident than when she entered the building, Clare followed the receptionist through a maze of work spaces, cubicles and offices. Then they came to a stop outside of a large mahogany paneled room with a "Board Room" sign on the door. It was surrounded by glass walls, revealing that there was indeed eight people seated around a large conference table waiting to meet her.

"Here we are. You're welcome to go right in. Good luck!"

The receptionist held the door open for her and smiled encouragingly as Clare made her way into the room.

Just about everyone stood up and came forward to shake her hand to introduce themselves. Their names went in and out of her head the moment she moved on to someone else.

However, she noticed that one person didn't come to greet her. That person was the only other woman in the room. An older, very distinguished looking woman who smiled at her, but just remained seated.

And it looked like this woman had some sort of remote control in her hand. Sure enough, when this woman pushed the button, curtains came down around the glass windows, shielding them from outsiders.

No one could now see what was going on inside the Board Room. Clare was secretly grateful for this, because if she didn't get the job, she didn't want everyone else to notice how badly it would hurt.

Wasting no time, the interview began.

Getting down to business, Clare instantly buried her nervousness. She drew upon her competitive instincts as a collegiate swim champ and let her natural outgoing personality take over. On the tough questions, she kept her answers simple, yet pithy while confidently responding to just about every question. On those questions she wasn't prepared for, she was able to address them with a bit of self-deprecating humor or with joke or two added in, which generated admiring smiles and even outright laughter from the guys in the room. However, the only other woman there didn't seem find her so funny.

Almost three hours went by in a flash and before she knew it, the meeting ended.

She knew for sure it had concluded when Grisham, the CEO stood up and said: "I'm going to need to leave shortly to catch a plane, but let me give you my initial thoughts right now. I'm impressed. I'm not going to speak for the rest of the leadership team, but in my opinion, your professionalism, intellect, achievements, and personality are off the charts. I think that you'd be a fantastic fit for our company as our head of HR. What do you think Lois?"

Lois was surprised and taken aback that she was being put on the spot in front of everyone.

But that didn't stop her.

And Lois being Lois, spoke her mind. After barely saying anything in the meeting, she now angrily snorted, "With all due respect, Grisham, I strongly DISAGREE!"

The CEO looked in her direction and frowned. "Is there something we're missing, Lois?"

With no hesitation, Lois perked up: "Yes, there is. Grisham, you know damn well that Drake deserves this job. He's in-house and we all know him."

So this is Lois, Clare realized. Maybe it was a good thing that she hadn't been in a one-on-one interview with her, because right now she looked pissed and seemed unimpressed with the way things had gone down.

Lois continued: "Why the hell you chose to fly this woman half way across the country is beyond me. I've listened closely and yes, she's bright, experienced, personable and just about everything else you just said. I'll give her that. But she doesn't know shit about our culture and how we do things here. She doesn't have experience with our HR policies and the systems that have taken us years to develop. And she's absolutely clueless about the major challenges issues facing our people and this company."

Grisham sighed. And the rest of the room gasped. Clare included.

There was a bitter, hard edge to Lois' voice.

He then chimed in, "Lois, of course, she doesn't know all of those things. She's an outsider. She can pick those up. Just like you did when you first joined the organization."

Clare sat there in her chair with her mouth open, both surprised and seething with rage as she listened to the CEO and Lois continue to debate each other back and forth, right there in front of her.

And it hurt her to think that this woman, who barely even knew her, could hate her so much.

Then there was the name Drake. This couldn't be the Drake that she'd just met. Could it? While Drake isn't the most common name in the world, it was probably just a strange coincidence and that name quickly left her mind. She was busy trying to get this job right now, and she had a feeling she was going to have to fight with this other woman to get it. The room quickly became loud and chaotic with everyone now erupting and chiming in with their opinions.

And all this arguing made Clare uncomfortable.

Finally, she had enough.

"EXCUSE ME! EXCUSE ME, PLEASE! Can I have your attention, please?" Clare yelled as she stood up.

She cut through all the loud noise with her own clear, yet commanding voice. And every head turned in her direction.

"I'm sorry, but I really don't think it's appropriate for me to be in here while this discussion is going on. Especially since there are such strong and differing opinions. I would like to excuse myself and wait outside in the lobby area until you conclude this part of your discussion…uh, if that's okay with all of you." She rushed to add that last part in there, because she didn't want to tick anyone off by sounding like she was trying to boss the group.

There was silence for a few uncomfortable seconds.

Then Grisham nodded and sighed heavily, "Yes, Ms. Hammond, that might be best. We're used to being open and having brutally frank and candid discussions around here on just about everything. And on HR matters in particular, I've encouraged Lois to push back and challenge us, and that's what we all love about her. But, you're right, for a moment, I think we all kinda forgot you were here. So thanks for having the presence of mind to get us refocused. I'll have Molly, my executive assistant, send you back in as soon as we're finished here. I want to apologize to you for seeing us, maybe at our worst."

Clare smiled and nodded her understanding, but didn't trust herself to say anything more. So she opened the door and slipped out quietly. They were back to arguing before the door could even close behind her.

IT SEEMED THAT EVERYONE LIKED HER, everyone that is except Lois.

And what if the rest of the leadership team decided to hire her, despite what Lois thought? That could be a big problem.

She was going to need Lois' help in getting up to speed on this new job quickly. And it could be awkward as hell between both of them in the beginning. Worst case, Lois could sabotage and undermine her just to prove that they made the wrong decision. After all, she apparently had someone else in mind for the job.

Clare sat in the lobby for almost an hour when the phone on the desk finally rang and she jumped. Molly, Grisham's assistant picked it up, but she spoke so low that Clare couldn't make out what she was saying from so far away.

After hanging up, she looked out at Clare. "They're ready for you. You can go back in now."

Pulling herself together, Clare swallowed hard and walked down the hallway back to the Board room.

# 9

## THE REALIZATION

Unable to control his curiosity, Drake wanted to see what his competition looked like. Who was this mysterious outsider that had been brought in to interview for "his" job?

The rumors and whispers around the office had finally gotten unbearable. So he went to talk to Molly, who as Grisham's executive assistant, always knew what was really going on in the company.

Molly was single and liked flirting with Drake. He knew she really liked him and he often used that to his advantage to squeeze her for information.

Today was no different.

"Hey, Molly, I absolutely love that necklace."

"Thanks Drake, it's great of you to notice. It belonged to my mom. I'm having dinner with her tonight and thought I'd wear it for her."

"Well, it certainly looks fantastic on you. Hey, I know you're busy. But can you tell me if all the rumors I've heard are true that an outside candidate is in to interview for Lois' job today."

"Yep. They're true. Grisham, Lois and the leadership team are in interviewing her in the Board Room right now with the curtains drawn."

"So, it's a woman, huh?"

"Yep, it is. And I'm glad, especially since Lois is leaving. We don't need to lose any women leaders around here. In fact, we need even more women at the top of the house in this place… "

And she quickly added: "…and, of course, more people of color too."

After an awkward pause, Drake gave her a knowing look and chimed in.

"I couldn't agree with you more, Molly. Now let me ask you something you may not want to answer. And I understand if you don't. Confidentially, what do you think of her chances of getting the job? It's no secret to anyone that I've been shooting for Lois' position for years."

"Uh, I'm not really sure, Drake. I do know that they took a break about fifteen minutes ago, and I heard one of the execs who was in the Board Room say that they were arguing right in front of her. He said Grisham and Lois were really going at it. A real knock-down, drag out argument. One of the worst they've ever seen. And the poor woman who was in from out of town to interview stood up and excused herself to come sit out here for over an hour."

DRAKE FELT ALL OF THIS WAS GOOD NEWS.

He knew Lois had his back, and perhaps that might actually be the reason for their conflict. He knew Lois would stand up for him, even to Grisham. Thinking about that made him smile and he stared off into the space right behind Molly's head. She thought his smile was directed at her and she grinned back, blushing and displaying her sparkling hazel eyes.

"Thank you, again, Molly. Appreciate it. If you hear anything else, let me know. You're a gem."

She blushed even more, "Will do."

Even though he liked Molly, that was as far as their relationship was ever going to go as long as she reported to Grisham. Even though she flirted with him all the time and clearly had the hots for him, they'd never go out. Casual sex was out of the question too. Too risky. He'd never want to date anyone at work. Besides he didn't have time. Had to get that promotion first. For now, Molly was merely a tool to help him get the information what he wanted.

And that's exactly what she'd just provided him.

Information.

Good information.

Suddenly, he spotted Grisham, Lois and the rest of the leadership team leaving the Board Room down the hall. Apparently, the meeting was over. He could now finally see who they were interviewing. But for some reason, no one else besides leadership team people had yet emerged from the Board Room.

But that was fine.

He decided that he would lay low and wait until the end of the day and approach Lois to get a firsthand account of what had happened. That would be the only sure way to put all of his fears to rest. Until then, there was nothing else he could do.

However, just as he was preparing to go back to his desk, he spotted an unfamiliar blonde woman just now coming out of the Board Room. She was some distance away and he could only see her from behind. He couldn't make her out clearly and could only see that she was casually chatting with Lois.

When she finally turned around to leave, and started walking towards him, he finally caught a good glimpse of her face.

He dropped that cup of coffee he'd been carrying around for hours.

It spilled everywhere on the marble floor, but he didn't care.

He now knew who that outsider was who was interviewing for Lois' job.

It was Clare.

# 10

## THE THIEF APPEARS

Drake couldn't believe it.

CLARE WAS THE THIEF THAT HAD BEEN BROUGHT IN TO STEAL HIS PROMOTION.

And she was now walking away from the Board Room towards him to reach the elevator.

As she approached, she stared directly at him.

He stared back.

Their eyes met.

She then walked right on by…without saying a word!

So he didn't either.

She continued to the elevator and waited for it to arrive as Drake stood by, unable to move, absolutely stunned. There were a thousand thoughts now floating through his head. None of them good. Once the elevator doors closed behind her with a muffled thump, the spell was broken and Drake shook his head to clear it.

The first thing he did was to clean up the coffee that he'd spilled. He went to the restroom to get some paper towels, then came back and crouched down to wipe up the mess, careful not to get any coffee on his pants.

As he cleaned things up, he remembered that Clare *did t*ell him she was in town was for a job interview. But like a dope, he never asked her much more about it. He was too damned consumed with himself.

Big mistake.

But regardless, there was no way in hell he was going to let her swoop in like a vulture and take his promotion. He'd worked too damn hard and too long, and he wasn't going to sit back like an idiot and get passed over.

He had to go talk to Lois.

HE NEEDED TO VALIDATE THIS and immediately made a beeline to her office. The door was closed, but he didn't care. He knocked on it rapidly, making it sound like he was going to hammer it down if she didn't answer.

"Come in."

Her voice had a sharp edge to it. And he knew that he needed to tread lightly, even though he was near a boiling point already. She jerked her head up from her laptop screen and saw who it was.

Her eyes widened as she recognized Drake.

She sighed heavily, could tell he was pissed and motioned that he should sit down.

"What the hell happened in there, Lois? I thought you had my back?"

He was doing his best not to lose his temper, but he knew that he wouldn't be able to keep his cool for long.

"Who told you I didn't? I fought like hell for you. In fact, if I wasn't retiring already, Grisham probably would have fired my ass after I went at him so hard in front of everybody. Even though we've worked together for years, you and I both know Grisham doesn't like being upstaged in front of anyone. But I didn't care. I spoke my mind."

"So Lois, have they made a decision?"

"Nope, not yet. There was too much raw tension in that room. I honestly don't know what they're going to do. Grisham finally told the candidate that we would get back to her shortly. But Drake, I'm gonna be honest with you, she was very impressive and everybody really liked her"

"What about you, Lois. Did you like her?"

"Honestly, she brings a lot to the party," Lois admitted. "She's personable, has a ton of charisma and phenomenal HR experience. She's an awful strong candidate. On the other hand, my big concern is that she doesn't know a damn thing about our company and our people. But as Grisham said, you wouldn't expect her to. Nevertheless, you're still my number one choice. You've worked too hard for this."

Lois fell silent, not knowing how this was all going to register on Drake's anger scale.

He soon let her know.

"If there's NOT been a decision made yet, that's good, right? When do I get my own interview? Have I been scheduled with the leadership team yet? Lois, you said you'd make sure I was interviewed last to give me a leg up on anyone else? Aren't they at least going to give me a shot at this job? Everyone knows I deserve it. I've sacrificed everything and now it looks like they're going outside just so they don't have to promote me. Is it because I'm black? I thought we were trying to improve diversity and inclusion in this company, there's not a single African-American on that damn leadership team."

With each question, his anger rose a notch, and by the end, he had his hands balled into fists and they were shaking.

Lois was getting more and more uncomfortable. She understood he was furious, probably with good reason. And so, rather than meet his anger with her own, she decided to remain calm and reason with him.

"Look Drake, I don't have all the answers for you. I wish I could put your mind at ease, but I can't. But I do know this. You will get your interview with Grisham and the full leadership team. Just like she did. I will make damn sure of that. And I will help you as much as I can. That you can count on too.

"NOW, DRAKE, AS FAR AS BEING BLACK IS CONCERNED, you know as well as I do that we've been working hard to increase the number of African-Americans and other under-represented groups throughout this company. You know that because you and I have worked for months on that together. So, I'm shocked you'd even bring that up. Sure, we still have an awful long way to go, but we're making progress. So the fact that you're black has nothing to do with this. In fact, it's probably to your advantage given that Grisham, himself, is pushing us for more diversity at the top of the organization. So that's not the issue. Okay?

"Let me tell what I'm really worried about, Drake. I'm much more concerned that they might not even include me in the final decision because of my outburst today with Grisham and the fact that I'm a lame duck and leaving anyway.

"Now I know none of this makes you feel good. But honestly, that's about all I can tell you right now. However, you're still in control. You're definitely going to have your interview. And you have an edge because everyone in that room knows you, respects you and has worked with you. But I'm not going to lie, based on what I saw today, you're going have to blow their socks off if you want this job!"

He nodded at her and his face clouded over.

There was nothing else to say.

And so he just lowered his head as he stood up and slowly turned to leave.

Deep down, he knew she was right.

And he was very concerned.

# 11

## DRAMA QUEEN

When Clare left that Board Room and her eyes met Drake's, of course she recognized him.

But she didn't know exactly what to say.

The stunned expression on his face said it all.

So she said nothing.

Neither did he.

But, when she boarded the elevator, she instantly put it all together. He was the "Drake" Lois referred to in the interview. And she instantly realized that the job promotion that he had been talking to her about at the stump by lake, was the same one that she'd just interviewed for.

SHE FELT TERRIBLE NOW and very confused.

By the time she reached the front entrance of the Nu Foods building she couldn't help but scream out, "Shit!" as she stomped her foot like an angry little child.

She then whistled, sharp and loud, and a faded yellow taxi detached itself from the flow of traffic to pull up in front of her. She opened the door with a yank, and the driver half turned around to say something to her, but he saw the look on her face and quickly changed his mind.

She barked out: "To the Sheraton just off Michigan Avenue! Now!"

And as soon as her door closed, the driver floored it, shooting the taxi into a gap that barely wedged it into the crowded flow of cars.

She stared out the window as the taxi took her back to the hotel. Emotionally torn, she was both happy and sad. Part of her was elated that the job interview was over. And another part of her just wanted to cry because of the situation with Drake that she'd now been thrust into.

Tears began welling up in her eyes.

She liked Drake, much more than she cared to admit. And it wasn't all because of his attractive looks and athletic body. She'd also felt a certain relaxing calm and ease when he talked to her in that strong, baritone voice. His enthusiasm and passion for his career was also very appealing and matched her own -- unlike her lazy, horrible ex-husband.

But now she found herself in the position of taking some of that passion that away from him.

The taxi pulled up at her hotel. She practically threw twenty bucks at the driver and jumped out. And then ran through the revolving doors, past the lobby to the elevator up to her room. Once inside, she flung herself on the bed and started crying uncontrollably.

WHY DID THIS HAVE TO HAPPEN NOW?

Why did this have to happen with him?

How do I deal with this?

Then it hit her, she pulled out her phone and left Liz a text message: *"Call me ASAP. Urgent!"*

Ten minutes later, Liz phoned back.

"Hey girl, whassup! Did you get that job offer yet? When you gonna invite me up to help you move to Chicago? Hey, just kidding. You said it was urgent. Talk to me, girl."

Clare explained everything that had happened over the last day or so.

Her second encounter with Drake by the lake.

The wild group interview in the Board Room.

That bitch Lois who wanted to sabotage her chances at getting the job.

And finally, her brief encounter with Drake afterwards.

She left out no details.

"Liz, I really don't know what to do. Damn it! I really like him. If only he had agreed to have drinks with me tonight, then maybe I would have had a chance to explain."

"CLARE, STOP BEING A DAMN DRAMA QUEEN and beating yourself up. It's not your fault. If I understand this right, it's not like you did all this on purpose. Right? It sounds like he never even mentioned the name of the company he worked for. And why would you even bother mentioning who you were interviewing with either? That makes no sense! You didn't hide anything to be sneaky. It seems to me to be just a minor detail that got overlooked."

"But girl, that's now a minor detail that has now exploded in both of our faces. What do I do?"

"Well, for one, have you tried to call him?"

"No."

"Well, what are you waiting on? Call him at work. Explain the situation and see what happens. Do it now. But before you do, there's one thing you need to think about first. You need to be prepared to tell him if you plan to take that job if they offer it to you. Are you ready to do that?"

"Yes, I am. That job is mine! But only if the money's right. I didn't fly five hundred fucking miles here to waste my time. From talking with the leadership team, I know it's a great job and a fantastic career move for me. And I just love this city. But they've got to show me the money. If they do that, I'm in! And I'll work everything else out from there."

"Good. Sounds like you got this nailed, Clare. So call him."

"But what if he's so pissed off he won't talk to me, then what?"

"That's easy. Go out tomorrow to your special spot by the lake and see if you can talk to him there."

"Girl, you're a genius! I'll keep you posted. Bye!"

With that Clare got up and jumped in the shower. She needed time to calm down, collect herself and plan her strategy for the call to Drake.

She grinned.

It was a simple plan, but it was brilliant. Liz had always come through for her and she did again.

She hurriedly threw on the hotel bathrobe and then grabbed her phone. Pulling the letter out of her purse, she scanned the last page until she found the number for the company's main receptionist. She punched in the digits on her phone and waited for someone to pick up.

"Thank you for calling Nu Foods, this is Jessica. How may I help you?"

Clare smiled. A friendly operator had to be a good omen, right?

"Hello, could connect me to Drake Williams, please."

She crossed her fingers, hoping that it would just be that simple.

"Who may I say is calling?"

Damn it. She'd hoped that she would be put straight through, but apparently that wasn't going to happen today.

"This is Ms. Hammond."

Maybe, if she was lucky, he might have forgotten her last name.

"Just a moment please while I get in touch with him."

Clare listened to the terrible hold music in her ear while she waited. It reminded her of those boring Broadway show tunes she hated. Rolling her eyes at the music, she found herself hoping and almost praying that he would answer the phone.

"Ma'am?" The woman's voice came back over the line.

"Yes?" She held her breath.

"He's not available right now. Would you like to me to put you through to his voicemail."

"Yes, that would be great."

"Okay, after the sound, you can leave him your message."

Beep.

*"Drake, this is Clare. I'll meet you tomorrow morning at the stump at the lake. Usual time. We really need to talk."*

And with that, she hung up.

It was now time for plan B.

Tomorrow she'd get up early and hope he'd show up at their special spot.

But she couldn't be sure he would.

# 12

## THE INTERRUPTION

Drake had been at his desk, thinking about his brief encounter with Clare as she left the Board Room.

But that wasn't all.

He was now getting prepared for his own upcoming interview with Grisham and the leadership team. Lois had clued him in on the questions they'd likely ask him and suggested some talking points for him to use. He had taken five pages of notes from their discussion and was studying them like he was cramming for a final exam.

All this was going on when the company operator had called him, telling him that he had a phone call from a "Ms. Hammond."

He'd paused for a moment to think about where he'd heard that name before, and then it hit him. It was Clare.

NO DAMN WAY was he taking a call from her!

He told the operator that he was tied up in a meeting and unavailable.

When he got the call, it interrupted him as he was already knee deep in concentration prepping for his interview. He needed to be on top of his game. The last thing he wanted right now was a distraction…especially from a woman who was trying her damndest to take his promotion away from him.

An hour later he picked up his voicemail with her message indicating that she'd meet him by the stump tomorrow.

He had to admit that she had balls. Not taking her call should have been a hint he wanted nothing to do with her. Unfortunately, she apparently hadn't seen it that way and wasn't planning on giving up.

Okay, he thought, I'll meet her tomorrow at the goddamn stump.

And we'll get this shit settled once and for all.

# 13

## THE CONFRONTATION

That morning, getting up out of bed was tough.

Drake wasn't looking forward to seeing Clare at the stump. As he walked towards the door, each step felt like his feet were encased in cement blocks, making it difficult for him to take steps.

He thought about not going. And then he remembered that just yesterday he'd been so eager to see her.

BUT TODAY WAS DIFFERENT.

When he arrived, Clare took charge and didn't waste any time. "Why didn't you want to talk to me yesterday at the office?" She started off innocently enough, but Drake wasn't buying it. There was something much more important brimming just under the surface, and he knew that.

"Are you serious? Look, there was nothing to talk about. Obviously, we're competitors for the same damn job. Frankly, I wish we had never, ever, ever met."

There, he'd told the truth and he'd injected enough malice into his words that he thought she might change her mind and just leave.

Unfortunately for him, she was not one to back down.

"Hey, look I came to apologize," she began. "I had no idea that the job interview I had was for the exact same position that you were telling me about. You didn't mention a company you worked for and I didn't mention who I was interviewing with. My bad. I'm sorry. They called me to come in without me even submitting a resume. I was hoping that we would still be able to be friends and sort of laugh this off as an unlucky coincidence."

"Unlucky coincidence?" he responded. "Is that what this is to you? This isn't some fucking game. I've worked my ass off for five long years preparing myself for this goddamn promotion. I've put my personal life on hold. And now when all my hard work is about to pay off, some blonde bimbo in a business suit shows up from Kansas City to throw a monkey wrench in my plans."

He wasn't done, "And as far as being friends is concerned, don't make me laugh. The only way that shit happens is that you take yourself out of the running for this job." He then crossed his arms over his chest and sat down on "his" stump like he was the principal and she was a naughty student that was getting punished for smoking in the bathroom.

She didn't expect him to be happy, but she was really stung by his words.

"I AM MOST CERTAINLY NOT A BIMBO IN A BUSINESS SUIT. That's insulting. I've been fighting that stereotype my entire business life. I've worked my ass off too. Let me tell you something you may not want to hear. If your company called me to come up here to interview, then they must have thought that they didn't have anyone in-house that was strong enough and with enough balls to be up to the challenge. How is that my fault if you don't fit the bill?"

She'd gone for the jugular.

She'd come here to apologize, but she wasn't going to be stepped on in the process.

Since her divorce, she would never again let any guy ever hurt or disrespect her. And being called a blonde bimbo, to her, was the ultimate insult.

The words that she'd flung at him must have hit him hard, because the smug expression that he'd had on his face was suddenly gone. His eyes seemed to spark with all the anger that he was holding inside, and the tension between them got even worse than what she thought it could be.

"My balls are fine. And I fit the bill just fine, too, thank you very much. Now, let me tell you something YOU don't want to hear, Ms. Hammond. What the CEO wants is another pair of legs to spread whenever he feels like it. How do you think Lois got that job in the first place? Did you notice she's the only woman on the leadership team? How do you think she got there? Why do you think she keeps her job? Do you plan on following in her footsteps?"

The smugness was back on his face, and his eyes flashed at her.

She had another insult ready to fling at him, but when his words finally sank in, she lost her comeback.

Could it really be true?

Is that how Lois got her job?

Is that what she needed to do to keep it?

Well, that was not something Clare was prepared to do in a million years. If that was how Nu Foods worked, then she wanted none of it.

"Lois doesn't strike me as the kind of person that needs to screw her way to the top. That's a load of crap. You're making all that up. You're lying!"

"Am I?" he said, staring at her, with a sinister grin on his face.

With that, she stood up. It was her turn to leave abruptly.

"Where are you going?"

"None of your damn business."

And with that she disappeared.

# 14

## MORE CONFRONTATION

Clare was shocked by what she'd heard from Drake. It was something that she would definitely have to validate before she could consider this job any further.

And that's what she intended to do.

At precisely nine the next morning, she showed up at Nu Foods. She sweet talked her way the past the security guard, who smiled and remembered seeing her the previous day.

She then sneaked on the elevator, took it to the 25th floor and asked around before someone finally directed her to Lois' office.

She knocked angrily on her door.

When Lois opened it, surprised she said: "Oh, it's you. What do you want? The job isn't yours yet, you know."

"Yes, I know that. But we need to talk. Right now."

Clare breezed by her and sat down in Lois' guest chair.

Stunned by her brazenness in just barging in, Lois had no choice but to close the door behind them rather than create an office scene that would attract everyone's attention.

"I need to ask you something and I really need you to be honest with me."

She was now staring at Lois like a deranged serial killer.

"What is this all about? Am I going to need to call security?" Lois said, picking up her phone.

"No, you won't. I really apologize for intruding on you like this. But I have to know. I was just talking to Drake, and he told me that you slept your way into this position. And that, if I got this job, keeping my legs spread for Grisham was going to be a requirement for keeping it. I need to know the truth. Is that the deal for this job?"

Putting down her phone, Lois stared at this much younger woman, with her eyes bugged out and mouth hanging ajar. She couldn't believe her ears.

"Are you shitting me? Hell no! I'm a happily married woman. And just how the hell do you know Drake, anyway. Hey, I don't care. That's beside the point. Look, if you'd done your home-work on Grisham, you'd know that he'd never do that. But that's beside the point too. I don't know what you're trying to pull here or what your goddamn game is…but I'm going to go talk to Drake and get to the bottom of this shit right now. And, if you're lying to me, you can say goodbye to ever setting foot in this company ever again. I will make damn sure of it. Now there, I've answered your stupid ass question, get the fuck out of here because I need to check this out. And I'll tell you this…if there is one grain of truth in what you're saying, I'm going to kick Drake's ass."

Lois all but shoved Clare out of her office, closing the door behind the two of them. She then stalked her way down the hall towards Drake's office.

Clare then turned around and hurriedly went in the other direction to the elevator. There was no way she was going to hang around and witness the fireworks.

When she reached the lobby, she stood there for a few minutes, thinking that she'd just made everything even worse for Drake. Perhaps he had only said what he did to scare her off of the job. Was that a real possibility? Even if it was, it was now too late. The damage was done. However, if he was lying, he deserved what was coming.

About fifteen minutes later, a very angry Lois ended her private conversation with Drake.

Things didn't go well for him.

HE CAME CLEAN.

He apologized to Lois, explaining that he had just met Clare a few days ago entirely by accident. He saw her leaving the Board Room after her interview and realized she was interviewing for Lois' job. It was all just a coincidence. But he admitted when they talked later, he lost total control of himself, reacted angrily and said those things to scare her off the job.

As Lois listened, she was beyond pissed. She saw a side of Drake she didn't recognize. An evil, devious side. He was always in control, ethical, never ruthless and untrustworthy.

Now for the first time, she had some misgivings about ever recommending him for her position.

And it bothered her.

A lot.

# 15

## BACK TO KANSAS CITY

Clare muttered to herself on the ride down the elevator from Lois' office.

She'd never been a snitch before, not even when she was a kid in school. So why had she immediately gone to Lois and ratted on Drake? Sure, she certainly needed to validate what he'd told her. But even so, she didn't feel good about doing this to him.

Anyway, it was time to move on.

It had been an exhausting three days in Chicago.

And it was time to get back home to Kansas City.

She looked at her watch and knew that she didn't have a lot of time. It was now noon. Her United Airlines flight home was scheduled for 7:30 pm that evening. However, she'd already scheduled a ride to pick her up at 4:30 at the hotel to catch her flight. And she'd have to go through the legendary Chicago rush hour too.

She'd be pushing it.

But there was one more thing she needed to do before she left Chicago.

She needed a swim.

She had been so busy, she couldn't remember the last time she'd been for a real dip in the water. And besides, maybe if she went for a swim, she could get her mind off things.

She went to her luggage and put on a real swimsuit this time, throwing on some shorts and a t-shirt over it. She also stopped in the deli in the hotel to pick up a sandwich.

Her destination: that stump by the lake. For days, she had been dying to jump in those beautiful waters. And she knew for certain that Drake was at work and wouldn't be there to disrupt things.

The sun was shining down on her as she jogged there. She had packed her sandwich, a towel, and some dry undergarments in a small bag. She laid everything out neatly, and shed her outer shorts and shirt to reveal her swimsuit underneath.

She took the clip out of her hair and tossed it onto her bag before she jumped in.

It felt so soothing and relaxing to be back in the water.

She lost herself in the waves and in thought just doing some casual back-stroking as the sun shined down on her face. However, as she floated in the water, her mind floated back to the situation with Drake.

As far as she knew, she was his only competition for his dream job.

But she deserved this opportunity too.

She could feel her heart racing and her thoughts spinning, but she couldn't downplay her anger. She'd always been in complete control of herself and her emotions, especially when she was in a business situation.

So why had she allowed things to get so far out of control with Drake today?

WHAT WAS IT ABOUT HIM that made it so easy for him to get under her skin like that? The only thing that she could come up with was the fact that she genuinely liked him a lot. "Liked" being in the past tense, for sure, now that he'd insulted her and tried to frighten her away from a great job…just because he wanted it for himself.

The more she thought about his behavior, the more she realized that she was the better candidate, anyway. If he could lose his temper like that with her because he was disappointed that she interviewed for his job, how would he handle much tougher, emotionally charged situations he'd face as the HR VP? Like selling senior management on a brand new HR strategy. Or firing poor performers. Or downsizing entire departments. Or handling sticky discrimination or sexual harassment situations involving senior people. Even though he seemed like a great guy…even a nice guy, at times…could he step up to the plate and manage these kinds of tough situations as the top HR leader at Nu Foods? She doubted it.

All this just convinced her further that she needed to go after this job, for herself, with a vengeance.

And if she got it, then she'd be his boss, and he would have to deal with it or she'd fire his butt.

On the other hand, if she didn't get the job, then she'd reassess things back in Kansas City and try to forget about this rude, sorry jackass of a man that had more mood swings than a pregnant woman.

She remained lost in thought until her stomach reminded her that she was hungry. She then emerged from the water, dried off, then spread the towel out on the ground and sat down to air dry and eat her sandwich.

When she was done, she packed everything up and glanced around quickly to make sure that no one could see her. She then then swapped her wet bikini for her dry undergarments, before slipping back into her shorts and t-shirt before jogging back to the hotel.

Once there, she packed her bags and prepared to meet her ride outside the hotel to catch her flight back to Kansas City. Despite everything that happened, she was hoping that she would hear from Nu Foods soon about the outcome of her interview.

They told her they would make a final decision in about a week or so.

And she couldn't wait.

# 16

## DRAKE'S INTERVIEW

The day after Clare returned home, Drake finally had his group interview.

He met with Grisham and the entire leadership team...*just like Clare did.*

His interview lasted over three hours...*just like Clare's did.*

The leadership team challenged him with some brutally tough questions....*just like they did with Clare.*

But his interview didn't go so well...*not at all like Clare's.*

He could tell.

The vibe just didn't feel good.

Even though he knew all these folks and had worked with many of them for years, their body language and facial expressions gave them away.

Blank stares greeted him as he responded to their questions.

His attempts at humor got no chuckles and fell flat.

Some of them crossed their arms and frowned as he spoke.

And one guy, Jeff, the head of Marketing, never looked at him at all. Instead, he spent the whole time subtly texting and checking email messages.

He couldn't wait to get feedback from Lois afterwards.

Lois wouldn't pull any punches. She'd give him the straight scoop.

And she did.

"Damnit, Drake you bored the shit out of the leadership team this morning. I confess, you almost put me to sleep too. You started out well. But after ten minutes, you had no enthusiasm whatsoever and you just lost them. You spoke in this robotic, monotone voice. And instead of prioritizing your accomplishments, you dragged us step-by-step through every single freakin' HR project you've had over the past five years."

"And that's not all," she continued angrily, "you used entirely too many buzzwords. You know Grisham hates that shit. For example, you kept talking about 'human capital optimization.' Just who the hell were you trying to impress? That's fancy talk that our overpaid consultants use when they want to slap us with a big bill for their services. What happened to simple words like 'people' or 'talent' or 'human resources' or 'workforce'? That's what our leaders understand."

Unfortunately for him, she wasn't nearly finished with her blunt feedback.

There was more.

"When Grisham asked you about what our HR strategy should be for the future. I thought you and I talked extensively about this. Again, you started off good. You mentioned that the HR strategy had to be linked to the business strategy. Now that was fine. But it went downhill from there. You gave no specifics. Yes, you mentioned things like engaging the workforce, bringing in diverse talent and developing our leaders. But they know all that stuff. They wanted to hear details…examples, specific new ideas that could help take Nu Foods to the next level. They didn't get that."

"But Lois—"

"Hey, don't interrupt me, I'm not done! Do you want my candid feedback or not?"

"Yes, I do."

"Then let me finish giving it to you!"

"Okay…okay…"

"Look, I'm just trying to be helpful. You know I'm in your corner and will always support you. But sometimes, you don't pick up on signals other people are sending you and you can be entirely too serious. And in the interview, you were too damn serious. Even when you tried to joke to lighten the mood, you never smiled yourself. Not one goddamn time. You interviewed like your cat just died. You weren't having any fun. Clearly a lot was riding on this. And the stress showed. Everyone knows you, respects the hell out of you and they were expecting you wow them. You didn't. Had you been more selective in what you said and put more passion in your voice about what you'd accomplished, it probably would have made more of an impact."

"Okay, Lois, I get it. My interview didn't go so well. To be honest, I felt some of this too. But I definitely didn't expect the reaction to be this bad. I'm very concerned now. What's the bottom line on all this?"

"Bottom line, it seemed like you ignored just about everything you and I talked about before the interview. And frankly, compared to that other candidate, Clare, you came across as boring, flat and not ready for prime time."

With that, he just sadly lowered his head.

LOIS THEN WRAPPED UP WITH THE CLINCHER, "I hate to tell you this, but this job was yours to lose. And I think you may have just lost it."

# 17

## THE OFFER

One week after she got home, Clare's phone beeped with a voicemail message from a number in Chicago she didn't recognize.

She tapped on her phone to listen to the message.

*"Hello, Ms. Hammond. This is Grisham Perry, CEO of Nu Foods, could you call me back when you get a chance. This is my cell number, so call me anytime. I have some great news I'd like to share with you."*

Her hand was shaking as she held her phone. She knew this was it.

She decided that she would call him back after she showered. It had been a tough day at work. And a long hot shower always calmed her down which was good because she didn't want to sound too overeager for this job. But this time, she was barely in the bathroom long enough to get her hair washed and her body wet before she came sprinting out, anxious to get him on the line.

She took several deep breaths while she held her phone out in front of her, blinking at it rapidly to keep the water from getting in her eyes. She quickly wrapped a towel around her hair, making it look like she had a beehive on top of her head before drying off her face and ears. She didn't want to get water on her phone. She punched in his number and waited. When he picked up, she had to clear her throat before she could speak.

"Hello, Mr. Perry, this is Clare Hammond. I received your message asking me to call back?"

"Oh, yes! Hi, Ms. Hammond. May I call you Clare? And please, please call me, Grisham – everybody in the company does. I've got some great news. I was calling to let you know we wanted to offer you the Vice President of Human Resources position. Everyone was extremely impressed and we believe you'll be quite an asset to our senior leadership team. I've got an evening meeting coming up in about an hour, so if you don't mind, let me get right to the point and give you a quick overview of our offer, starting with the total compensation package. I have the numbers jotted down right here and then I'll have Lois get out the written offer letter to you both by e-mail and express mail with all the details. Is that okay...? Hello?"

"Yes! Sorry. I got distracted for a moment. This is great news. Sure. Please continue, Grisham."

"No problem."

Clearly reading from notes, he then went through the total pay package of her offer. It represented a 30% increase in her base salary, a bonus target which was 25% more than she was making right now plus restricted stock options, which she didn't have at all at her current firm. In addition, a sign on bonus of $80,000 was hers after her first month, but she'd have to pay it back if she left the company within eighteen months.

"Clare, what do you think of our offer?"

Inside she was bubbling over with excitement. But she didn't want to appear overly enthusiastic and tip her hand, so she played things cool in case she needed to negotiate the offer further.

"Sounds interesting. However, Grisham, I do have some questions."

"I thought you would. Fire away."

"What about relocation? The cost of living in Chicago is much higher than in Kansas City."

"I don't think that'll be an issue. As we remember, you're currently renting not owning, correct?"

"That's right."

"No problem. We'll handle all the expenses of relocating and moving you from Kansas City to Chicago and we'll provide an allowance for the first year to cover the increased cost of living here. Now I don't have all the nitty-gritty details at my fingertips right now, but they will all be spelled out in writing in the detailed offer letter we'll get out to you right away. The letter will also describe our health insurance program, benefits and numerous other perks that go with the job that I think you'll be impressed with. And you should feel free to call either me or Lois if anything is unclear."

"So what do you think, Clare?"

She was going to continue playing her cards close to the vest. "That sounds fair. I don't have any additional questions about the comp and benefits part of the offer, right now. But I may have some more once I see the written offer letter."

"Sure, I understand. That makes sense."

"Can I be honest with you, Grisham?"

"By all means."

"I am very concerned about Lois. Sounds like she had some huge reservations about me when I interviewed and she seemed to have had another in-house candidate in mind. How does she feel about me coming on board?"

"Great question. I knew you'd ask. You should know that Lois is an institution around here and everyone respects her. I value her input tremendously and she's both a terrific business leader and HR leader. At your interview, Lois was being Lois. If you accept this job, you've got some big shoes to fill. No doubt about it. But let me be brutally honest. She's retiring. She won't be here. As CEO, I have an obligation to consider her input and the rest of my team's, and I've done that. But the final decision rests with ME to select the candidate that I believe will lead our HR function the best and help our company win in the future. And Clare, that candidate is YOU."

He continued.

"Frankly, in many ways you remind of Lois. You're strong, know your stuff and you're perceptive about people. And you're a leader. The three hours or so we spent interviewing you was a pressure cooker. That was intentional. You'll face much tougher situations in this job. I liked how you dealt with the questions we asked and the way you handled our group when things got a little heated. And all our reference checks we did on you back this up too. You're exactly what Nu Foods needs. I want someone in HR who is not afraid to take a stand and express their point of view – even if they're wrong. Sometimes when you straddle the fence, you sit on a spike. That's what I like about Lois. And what I like about you."

Still not done, he was on a roll and had more to say.

"HOWEVER, LET ME LAY ALL MY CARDS ON THE TABLE. There's one thing that's disappointed me. We don't have enough diverse people at Nu Foods. I've gotten on Lois consistently about this. It's the one big thing in HR both she and I have both have failed at. Our culture is stale and out-of-date – and we're getting our asses handed to us by the competition.

"We have too many inflexible white males here, especially on my leadership team. They aren't embracing change and evolving fast enough. I'm saying this as a conservative, middle-aged white man myself who's been in business all my life. But, believe me, I can see the writing on the wall.

"Our business will suffer," he continued, "if we don't bring in more people with diverse viewpoints to challenge us. We need more women. More people of color. I don't care what their sexual orientation or politics are either. I just want the best and brightest from all over the world with crazy new ideas that can shake up our culture and help us innovate. This is an absolute necessity to take our company to the next level. It's something I'm hoping to work with you on, that you can really help us with.

"Are you up to that challenge, Clare?" Grisham said smoothly, trying to get some indication of her interest in the opportunity he laid out.

"I most certainly would be up to it... that is, if I decide to accept this job," she responded confidently, but still staying neutral about her interest.

"Okay. I understand. You're not ready to commit yet. I get it. So let me get back to Lois because that was your question. I know both of you didn't hit it off at first. However, I think you'll be surprised. She has come around quite a bit since you were last in here. In fact, believe or not, a few days ago, she barged in my office and demanded that I make you this job offer immediately. She didn't want us lose you. When I asked her why, we had a very long and candid conversation. She talked about how you confronted her in her office and how she admires your courage and spine."

"Grisham, how specific was Lois about what she and I talked about?"

"She told me everything. Yes, she even told me about the crazy rumor you had heard about how she had to turn tricks and do sexual favors in order to rise to her current position. She didn't tell me who told you that, even though I pressed her hard to reveal her source."

"I can't reveal that to you that either."

"That's fine. Your job is to preserve confidences. I respect that. But let me very blunt about what you discussed with Lois. Screwing the boss is not a requirement of this job. For one, I'd never ever do that and I'd fire anyone in the company who did – right on the spot!

"Personally," he continued, "I keep my romantic life and work life separated. I've been in a committed relationship with my partner, Andrew, for five years. In fact, I'm surprised that in your online search about me and our company, you didn't uncover that fact that I'm gay...maybe you did...since Andrew and I have been public about our relationship for over three years. A few years ago it was big news. But the buzz has died down. It's no longer such a novel thing since Tim Cook at Apple and other CEOs have come out. My relationship was also part of a big interview I did with the Wall Street Journal awhile back and so everyone in the company knows about it."

"Grisham, believe me, I did my homework on the company. The fact that you're gay wasn't and isn't important to me. If it was, I wouldn't have come in for the interview in the first place. And it won't be a factor in my decision whether to accept the job."

"That's good! But you should know, before you decide to come, that it has been a factor in *other people's* decisions. When that article came out, two of my top people left because they didn't want to work in a company headed by a CEO in the LGBTQ community. That hurt me and let me know there's still a bias against certain people in corporations, including ours.

"I hear the whispers and rumors any time I'm staying late to meet one-on-one with any male member of our leadership team. And anytime a man is promoted into a leadership role, the gossip is that he slept with Grisham to get there. This is all very frustrating. That's another reason why we need more diverse, non-traditional, progressive thinkers here -- to help change our culture and erase these negative perceptions about our business."

She chimed in, "But those perceptions are all so ridiculous and unfair to you, and–"

He interrupted, "I know it is. YOU know it is. But people are people. And that's our culture right now. The one you'll be stepping into. That's why I want to be totally upfront and transparent with you about all this. I also want to encourage you to talk to Lois and check all this out further with her. I have no doubt she'll be brutally honest. Look, we're not perfect. But we have nothing to hide. If you accept this job, I want you to come in with your eyes wide open about what a great opportunity this job is...but you need to know what the HR challenges will be too.

"Any other questions, Clare?"

"Grisham, wow. I'm blown away by how open and candid you've been with me. It's my turn to be honest. There's a lot here for me to process. I'm going to need some time. Financially, this is an incredibly, incredibly generous job offer. Thank you. I'd typically negotiate for a few more dollars...but, that would be an insult to you and Nu Foods, based on everything you've just told me. I'd just like a few days to think things over.

To look over the written offer, if that's okay? This is an important decision for both of us. Should I get back to you or Lois with my decision?"

"Get back to me directly. But again, don't hesitate to call Lois about the details of the offer and feel free to discuss anything with her...and I mean, *anything,* including everything we've talked about. I hope you will consider our offer favorably and that you can let me know as soon as you can. Speaking on behalf of Nu Foods, again, we'd love to have you join our team."

"Thanks Grisham. I'll be back in touch in a few days. Have a terrific evening."

"You too. Take care."

She then hung up.

And just sat there.

Completely stunned.

Trying to digest and let everything she'd just heard sink in.

Then she got up and started to dance around the living room until her towel fell off. Yes, it was juvenile, but she was just so excited that she couldn't help it. She hastily picked up her towel and went back to the bedroom to soak all this in and to immediately call Liz with the news.

AS GRISHAM PROMISED, the written offer arrived the next day by email and a second copy by same-day express mail.

She read it over carefully and had her attorney review it too.

She also called Lois with more questions about the offer and discussed her candid talk with Grisham. They talked for over an hour and things could not have gone better. Lois was pleasant, candid and helped convince her that this was a fantastic opportunity she should not refuse.

And she didn't.

Exactly 72 hours after her last conversation with Grisham, she called him back and accepted the offer. They agreed she'd start in two weeks. And that she'd be staying at the same Sheraton hotel in downtown Chicago on an interim basis, until she found permanent housing.

She was overjoyed!

# 18

## IT'S OFFICIAL

Meanwhile, at home, Drake was in a foul mood because earlier that day Lois told him that there was a good chance he'd blown his interview.

In disgust, he threw his empty glass against the wall of his kitchen, watching it shatter into dozens of sparkling pieces. The sparkles of broken glass reminded him of how the sun would hit the waves of Lake Michigan near his stump.

And it forced him to think of Clare.

He couldn't get his interview or her out of his mind. He was kicking himself for trying to scare her away from the job by lying to her about what was required. He felt terrible about what he had done. Now he was home alone, drinking Scotch by himself to drown his sorrows and to forget about the horrible week he'd just had.

He sighed heavily and went to get the dust pan out from under his kitchen sink. He mindlessly swept up the glass pieces.

Then he grabbed a new glass, and steadily drank glass after glass of Scotch until his bottle was empty.

His vision started to blur, and he was unsteady on his feet as he made his way down the hallway to his bedroom. He dropped on the bed on top of his blankets and passed out immediately. Sinking down into the oblivion was the kindest thing that had happened to him all day.

The next morning, he was still asleep during the time that he should have been awake for his run to the stump. But he snored right through his beeping alarm clock. Luckily for him, he had two alarms set. One was for getting up to go run. And the other one was set so he would know when he had to leave the house in order to still get to work.

When the second alarm sounded, it had a different sound to it. It was louder and more insistent. Drake's eyes slowly began to flutter. He blinked the sleep away, turning his head to look at the time. It took a minute or two for it to sink in. It was 9 am. He was beyond late. He jumped off the bed, realizing two things at the same time.

One, was that he was still in the same clothes that he'd worn yesterday.

And two, he stank of Scotch.

It was going to be a long day.

Even though he rushed through a shower and put a little extra cologne on, he could still smell the Scotch on himself and he wasn't under any illusions that others wouldn't be able to also.

He caught a taxi and arrived at work. He stumbled through the lobby and tried to wedge himself in the corner of the elevator. He pretended not to notice how the other two people in the elevator with him flared their nostrils when he came in. It was as if they thought they knew what they were smelling, but wanted a second whiff before they confirmed it for sure.

When he got to the 25th floor, he hurried to his office, hoping none of the higher ups would see him.

He hadn't been there more than ten minutes when someone stopped by.

He couldn't tell who it was because his eyes were scrunched shut and his vision blurry.

"Your eyes are red and looks like you have a headache. And from what I can smell, maybe even a hangover. Maybe you should just go home? I don't think that I've ever seen you wasted and hung over before."

That voice belonged to Lois.

"No," replied Drake. "I'll be alright. I rarely ever drink and it only took one bottle of Scotch to get me this messed up. Besides, I think you're here to tell me something that I'm probably not going to like."

Lois gave him a look of disgust, still angry about how he had lied about her.

And then she unloaded.

"I'm sorry to have to tell you this, but it's official. You didn't get the job. It went to Clare Hammond. She'll be starting two weeks from now on Monday with me so I can begin to bring her up to speed on what we're working on. Can I trust you to be your usual hard working self when she arrives? Or am I going to have to force you to take some of your vacation days?"

She was looking at him now like the mother of a naughty child.

"I won't be a problem. I'll be back to normal by then and I'll be professional. But don't expect me not to harbor at least a little bit of bitterness. But I'll do my best." His voice had a rough edge to it.

Lois nodded, "Sure, I understand. But...there's one more thing..."

"There's more?"

"When she shows up, I'm going to need you to work directly with her for her first week or so. I'll be with her for her first day, but then I'll be gone for the rest of the week or so on a confidential special project for Grisham. I'll also be making the rounds of the factories and sales offices to say my goodbyes personally to some of the folks in the field that have helped me over the years. And I need you to step in to help Clare out, while I'm gone, on top of everything else you're working on. Think you can do that for me?"

The look of pure horror that he gave her made her have second thoughts about her request. But there was no one else that she could ask because no one else knew her job better than Drake did.

"Sure, Lois. No problem. I'll cover things for you here. Just like I've always done, until you get back," he said sadly.

As Lois turned to leave, he realized he was in no condition to work or deal with any clients or HR issues. "Hey, wait. Lois, on second thought, I'm going to take the rest of the day off. I feel terrible."

"That's a great idea. Go ahead and get out of here. Dry out and rest up. I'll see you Monday."

"Okay, Lois. See you then."

# 19

## DINNER AT SIMON'S

On her last official day at Allaco Beverages, twenty of Clare's colleagues treated her to a going-away dinner at Simon's, the best restaurant in Kansas City.

Liz flew in from Los Angeles to join in the group celebration and to also spend a couple of days with her best friend to help her pack up for her move.

At dinner, there was a gigantic cake and plenty of laughs, tears and drinks to go around. Everyone took turns roasting Clare, while describing how great she was to work with. Everyone, that is, except her direct boss who didn't come.

The CEO of Allaco even unexpectedly dropped in for a few minutes to say a few brief words and offer his best wishes for her in Chicago. As he departed, he bent over and whispered in her ear that he really respected her work and that if she ever needed to return to the company to just call him, personally.

Silently she wondered where all his appreciation was before she decided to resign. For a few seconds there she briefly reconsidered if she should leave at all. But then she quickly remembered the extraordinary career opportunity waiting for her in Chicago – and that her boss didn't even have the courtesy to show up here on her final day – which instantly erased any thoughts she had about changing her mind and staying put.

Nevertheless, Clare was blown away at all the recognition and appreciation everyone showered her with. Now, all she needed was Liz to drive her drunk ass home later.

This was certainly going to be a night to remember.

As she and Liz rode back to her apartment afterwards, the thoughts of Drake floated back into her mind and she sighed and frowned.

"What's wrong?" Liz asked.

"I don't know, I was just thinking…about Drake. I'm not quite sure if I took this job in spite of him, or just because it was an excellent opportunity to further my career. But now, it doesn't matter. I'm now going to be his boss and that's not something I'm looking forward to."

"Clare, the point is you earned that job all on your own. You deserve this, girl. You have nothing to be sorry about."

"I know. But…I'm not looking forward to working with Lois during her last few weeks either. She sure sounded nice over the phone when we last talked. But she's leaving and has all the power. She could screw me over in my first few days if she really wanted to. But it's a necessary evil, I guess. You know, part of me wants to work things out with Drake. Liz, I still like him, even though he said terrible things to me in order to chase me away from this job. But, I've seen the other side of him too, a warmer side, someone that I'd really like to get to know better."

"Girl, you'd better be careful. You're his boss now. I know you're horny, hard up and haven't slept with anybody for awhile. But you don't want to get your meat where you get your bread. You know what I'm saying?"

They laughed.

"Besides, what if he doesn't want to work it out with you? You still have to be cordial towards each other at work, right? If he can't handle that, you might have to fire his butt. Right?"

"Right. I guess…," she sighed heavily.

As she and Liz drove up to her apartment, they both got out.

She'd worry about how to deal with Drake later, tonight had been a fantastic celebration.

And a night she'd always cherish.

# 20

## CROSSING THE LINE

Two weeks after his interview, Drake went on his 5 a.m. run to his favorite spot.

When he arrived, he saw the now familiar, blonde shapely figure sitting on the stump. This time wearing a bathing suit.

He was hoping that she wouldn't be here today, and it seemed like all of his luck had run out. She turned to face him, and he turned to leave.

"Wow. Didn't expect to see you here Clare."

"Yeah, I'm just here for a quick swim."

"Monday is your first day on the job, right?"

"Yep, it is. Just moved into the Sheraton yesterday. It's just temporary until I find something permanent. My friend, Liz helped me pack back in Kansas City and then flew all the way in from LA and helped me move in."

She paused, before making her next statement.

"Are we going to have a problem at work? Is that thing that happened between us going to affect our working relationship?" Clare asked coldly.

"Look, I'm sorry. I shouldn't have lied to you. I apologize. I'm all in. I really want to make this work with you. But...but...it still stings a little bit about how you came in and got my job. And...."

He knew he should just shut up and just leave. But after the last few weeks, he needed an outlet for his frustration, and this was going to be it.

Now her face contorted in rage as well. And even though both of them knew that it would be safer to just walk away, they'd both been hurt to a point where they each wanted some kind of revenge.

"Excuse me?" she said, no longer able to hold in her anger. "I thought we talked all that out the last time we met. I told you before I had nothing to do with this! What more do you want me to say? Your company worked through a headhunter to find me in Kansas City and paid for me to fly out here for a job interview. How the hell is any of this my fault? Also, Lois and Grisham made it clear to me that the company really wants African-Americans in senior spots, so you had a built-in advantage over me to start with. Besides, if they wanted you at any point in time, why would they pick me?"

She then stood up, took a battle stance, crossing her arms over her chest and glared at him so hard that sparks seemed to be shooting at him from her eyes. She could tell her comment had hit home with him.

"Clare, I'm sorry. You know, I've been doing Lois' job every time that she goes on business trips – and my job too! I know her job like the back of my hand. It's all just a little frustrating. But you're absolutely right. It's not your fault. I shouldn't be taking all this out on you. I DID have the edge and blew it. Like I said, I'm all in. I guess I'm just venting a little bit. I'll try to do everything I can to make things go smoothly for you."

"I would really appreciate that, Drake. Thank you. Frankly, you know the organization and I don't. And I'm going to need all your help and more. Lois had mentioned that you'd be my main point person to help get me up to speed, while she takes her last business trip for the company. I hope that doesn't complicate things for us."

"It won't Clare," he said recognizing he had no other choice.

"That's good to hear. In return, I'll do anything I can to help you with your career too. Believe me, I was in your shoes at my

76

last company when an outsider was hired as my manager. I know it can tough to deal with. But I want to help. In fact, I had one interesting thought I think you might like..."

"What's that?" he said as his face perked up a little.

"Well, I know you and Lois are very close. And, if you're game, we can pick up where she left off from a career development standpoint and discuss some ways to add more growth and excitement to your current role."

"Now that would be good, Clare. I'd appreciate that. Do you have anything in particular in mind?"

"Yep, I do, believe it not. I don't know if you're interested, but there are two seminars I had planned to go to in New York three weeks from now. I can't go now, since starting a new job is the wrong time for me to be out of the office. But I'd love to have you attend in my place. The sessions are full and already paid for. They both cover global best practices for attracting and recruiting diverse talent for mid-sized companies. I thought you could go and bring back any fresh ideas to Nu Foods that you think we could potentially use. Perhaps I could help you present the best ones to Grisham and the leadership team."

"Wow. That's pretty generous. I haven't been to an HR seminar in ages. Been too busy. You'd be willing to do that for me?"

"Sure. It would allow you to expand your knowledge in an area that's at the top of Grisham's priority list -- and it would boost your value at the same time. **I'm a firm believer that from a personal development standpoint, you've got to treat yourself like a blue-chip stock. If you're not increasing your HR skills and your value all the time, you become like a stock that's declining in price that no one wants to invest in or have in their portfolio.**"

"Clare, good point. And I really like that analogy."

"There's another thing I've thought about too. How about this? What do you think about spending a day at Elementrix? They're a small high tech firm in Kansas City. They're doing amazing things with AI -- that is, artificial intelligence -- to save money and improve employee productivity. I'm not sure but I think there may be a couple of areas at Nu Foods, where we can apply what they're doing. Clark Haynes, their Chief HR Officer is one of my mentors, and he invited me there to visit next month to see what they're doing. But again I probably shouldn't be away for awhile. But what if you were to go down there in my place, meet with him and his team and check things out to see if there's anything there we can apply at Nu Foods? What do you think?"

"I'd like that. You know, I was just reading some intriguing stuff about AI and it would be awesome to see someone actually using it in the workplace with actual employees."

"Awesome, I'll give Clark at Elementrix a call and get the two of you connected. And I'd really encourage you to build a relationship with him too. He's a phenomenal guy. Been in HR for thirty years, funny as hell and one of the smartest guys I know. But he's also humble and easy to talk too. **His advice has been indispensable to me in my career and is one of about eight mentors that I rely for help.**"

"Eight mentors? You're kidding me," Drake said in disbelief.

"No, I really believe in the power of mentoring. I have about eight. And that just a rough guess. It could be one or two more. But you sound surprised. How many do you have?"

"If I count Lois, that's it. She's my only one. I've been buried at work so much I haven't had a chance to build many mentoring relationships, even though I know I should."

"Drake, I can understand you're busy. So am I. **But take my advice on this, those mentoring relationships are more important than you know. They really come in handy if you find yourself struggling with a tough HR issue. Or if find yourself on the street without a job and need referrals or job leads. Those are the times your mentors and other relationships are indispensable. I consider my mentors a critical part of my network that I treat as an ongoing investment in my future. These are folks I try to talk to at least two to three times a year. And every time I talk to them, I try to figure out ways I can *help them*. Sometimes I can and sometimes I can't. But that's what really makes these relationships work, they go both ways and they benefit me and them.**"

"In fact," she continued, "one of my contacts is the headhunter that called Grisham and referred me for the Nu Foods job. Apparently, both of them worked together at Quaker Oats years ago and Grisham respects him a lot. **I never would have learned about this job if it hadn't been for him. I only share all this to emphasize the importance of nurturing and growing relationships, both with multiple mentors and lots of others as well. Take it from me, it can really help your career and allow you to bring new insights to your job too.**"

"Hmmm..." he pondered, now stroking his chin. "That's deep. I've never heard that perspective on mentoring and relationship building before. Don't get me wrong. I'm not naïve. I'm in HR and I know that stuff is important. But this is the first time it's really been laid out to me in just that way. Thanks."

"You're welcome."

They continued exchanging ideas back and forth about more exciting potential growth and development possibilities for Drake. And his entire mood changed.

As did hers.

And an amazing thing happened. Each idea she proposed slowly and subtly caused both of them to step forward towards each other. And before they knew it, their faces were mere inches apart.

Suddenly, both of them fell silent staring at each other.

And Drake's eyes followed the curve of her face down to her lips. They looked so full and soft. He had long imagined what it would be like to kiss them. And so he lunged forward, mashing his lips against hers.

Clare's arms came up to his chest, initially to push him away. But instead, she knotted the material of his running shirt, pulling him even closer to turn their touching lips into a deeper, more passionate kiss. The two of them were already in a private place, but all of their surroundings seemed to fall away as they got lost in each other's arms.

Two minutes passed.

When they finally unlocked their lips for air, Clare smiled at him...and lowered her eyes.

When she took a glance up, he surprised her with a sad, confused look on his face.

"Clare, I'm so sorry. I crossed the line. I really shouldn't have done that. But I confess, I've wanted to do that since we first met and I just couldn't resist. But that's not fair, especially to you. You're my boss now. Forgive me. I lost my head. I don't want to make things awkward between us at work. I've worked hard for my job and I like it. And I especially like those ideas you've come up with, they're exciting."

And with that he started backing away from her and then walking away slowly.

"Wait, Drake, let's talk."

Embarrassed and looking over his shoulder as he walked away, he said: "There's really nothing to talk about. This just doesn't feel right. I'll see you in the office on Monday."

"But wait…"

Not heeding her voice, he kept walking.

She didn't follow.

After a few moments, tears welled up in her eyes.

After that kiss, it seemed that he'd been thinking along the same lines that she had. But he was right. Things had, indeed, now gotten very complicated and it *was* going to be awkward between the two of them at work.

Part of her liked that kiss immensely and she wanted more. But another part of her knew a romantic relationship with Drake was something she didn't need right now. After all, she was starting a new job, in a new city at a new company. She was his boss. And was definitely going to need his experience, knowledge and support to guide her. And frankly, she needed those things more than anything romantic. Their situation was going to be tough enough. She didn't need it to get more complicated.

At least right now.

However, Monday was her first day. And she had a packed schedule of meetings planned with Lois, Grisham and lots of other key people.

If she was lucky, she wouldn't have to see Drake at all.

# 21

## MOM'S WISDOM

The weekend was sheer torture for Drake.

He couldn't get his mind off that kiss.

He knew that he shouldn't have initiated it. But he'd acted on impulse, but after it happened, he knew he had to get the hell out of there.

Clare had yelled out to him and clearly wanted to talk about it.

But he didn't.

However, he knew walking away as he did didn't solve anything. It was perhaps only making matters worse. But it was the only thing that he could think of in order to avoid totally losing control over his emotions and to keep his own growing romantic feelings about her in check.

But she'd be in for her first day on Monday.

So he didn't have long time to figure out a strategy for dealing with all this at work. And at this point, HIS MIND STARTED RACING AROUND IN CIRCLES.

Even though that kiss happened before she officially started, that didn't mean that she wasn't still his boss. She most certainly was. However, what would happen if this got out?

What would the people at work think? The rumor mill at Nu Foods was treacherous.

How would the higher ups react? Grisham and Lois had recently fired an Engineering VP for sexual harassment and used the incident to reiterate the company's zero tolerance policy.

Was he at risk for getting fired too? What if Clare filed a lawsuit against him alleging unwanted advances or sexual harassment? If she did that, he was going to be screwed royally for the rest of his professional life.

Would she do that?

Nah...she wouldn't.

Would she?

Nope, he finally reasoned.

Besides she had kissed him back. She definitely embraced him and returned his kiss -- and it wasn't just a peck on the lips. It was a long, deep romantic kiss. And consensual.

Worst case, if she took him to court, and made a stink about it, it would be her word against his. And he never erased her voicemail. The one that said: *"Drake, this is Clare. I'll meet you tomorrow morning at the stump by the lake. Usual time. We really need to talk."* This was potentially damning evidence if she ever wanted to press her case legally.

While he couldn't imagine her doing this, she *could* make up a reason to fire him.

Or even demote him.

His mouth dropped open at that thought.

Nah...she wasn't that type of person. Was she?

She couldn't! It was bad enough that she'd taken the job from him, but to fire or demote him completely? No, that was just a bridge too far.

Still, he didn't know her well enough to be able to judge her next move. So he did the only thing that he could do. He sat at home, continuing to play mind games with himself.

MAYBE HE COULD AVOID HER altogether on Monday. Yes, that's it! That's what he'd do. He knew she'd have a busy first day, so he definitely could avoid her. Sounded like a plan.

Just then his phone rang.

Without checking the number, he put the phone to his ear.

"Hello. Who's this?"

"Hi son. How are you?" The voice was older and sweet, with a slight southern accent.

"Oh…hey, mom. Didn't know it was you. How are things going? Is everything okay?"

"Oh, everything's just fine, sweetheart. I just thought I call you to check in on things. You never call us. We miss you. And frankly, we'd love to talk to you more often, but you're never at home. You're always busy at work and we don't like to bother you there."

"I know. I know. I'm sorry. How's dad?"

"Your dad is just fine. He's out in the garage with one of his buddies fixing an old car. As soon as he gets cleaned up, we're going out for sushi and maybe a movie later."

"That's great. Things at work have been a little more hectic than normal. That's why I haven't called. I've been burning the candle at both ends. But, don't worry about me, things will clear up soon."

"Drake, tell me…what's wrong?"

"Why do you think something's wrong?"

"Son, you don't sound so good. I can tell by the tone of your voice and by the abrupt way you answered the phone. Tell me what's going on?"

She might have been seventy-two years old, but that woman was still perceptive, on top of things and street smart – just like she was when she taught high school science back in Detroit. He had strong suspicions that she was the one that he'd gotten all of his smarts from. But his work ethic, that definitely came from his dad.

"Mom, no matter how I try, I can never put anything over on you. You always could tell when something wasn't quite right with me."

"That's right. Now what's the matter?"

He chuckled, then took a deep breath.

And he slowly told her the whole story.

He began by telling her how he met Clare at his secret place that he'd run to every morning. He described how they'd hit it off. Then he explained how he found out she was interviewing

83

for his dream job. He then stumbled over his words as he explained, in the least amount of detail possible, about how tried to chase her away from even considering the job, by lying about what Lois had to do to keep it. Then he'd told her how he and Clare had gotten into the huge argument at the stump a few hours ago that had led to their first kiss.

"Kiss! A kiss? Did I hear you right? A kiss?"

"Yeah, mom, a kiss."

"Hmmmpf..." she grunted in disbelief.

Then he told her they finally decided to hire Clare, not him. And she'd now be his boss and they'd have to work together.

That was all he felt comfortable revealing at this point. And he let out a deep breath he hadn't even known he was holding.

"Wow. Son, you've been busy. I see why you haven't called. There's just never a dull moment with you, is there?"

She had a teasing tone to her voice, but he winced, knowing that it was true.

"Mom, it just feels good to talk and get this stuff off my chest. There's not a lot of people I can really let my hair down with these days. I've been working so hard. I have absolutely no social life. I'm not in contact with any of my buddies from school. Everything is work, work, work. I appreciate you just listening. This is all so frustrating. They've stolen the promotion I've worked so hard to get. I feel like I've let you and dad down. I feel like I've let myself down. I don't know what to do."

After a long pause, she spoke.

"Let me give you some advice. You're a grown man now, so you can ignore me if you want. But I know you better than you know yourself, ever since I first put a diaper on that little black butt of yours. So I want you to listen to me."

"Okay, mom, go ahead and let me have it. Say what you need to say. You're going to do it anyway."

He winced and closed his eyes, picturing her standing in the kitchen leaning against the counter, with the phone in her hand.

"Son, as far as your dad and I are concerned you are a success already. The only thing we want from you now is to give us some grandbabies. But careerwise, you don't have to prove anything to us. I know you wanted that promotion, because for you, it's a matter of pride. I understand that. But you know, I'm a religious woman and I have faith that everything happens for a reason."

She was a committed, lifelong Southern Baptist.

But she knew he was not.

He'd stopped going to church as a teenager after she quit forcing him to. And she did her best not to bring her faith into conversations with him because she knew he'd just roll his eyes and tune her out. And then they'd argue because his reactions would offend her. And she would start preaching at him more, which then would offend him even more. And it would become an endless circle of anger.

Knowing all this, she chose her words carefully.

"You know something, maybe there's a much deeper reason you didn't get that promotion. What if you were destined for something bigger and better than just that job at Nu Foods? What if there is an even better job out there that the universe hasn't revealed to you yet. I have faith and believe that you were given your brains for a reason. And I believe if you just keep your eyes open for right opportunity, it will present itself to you.

"Now, as far as that woman you kissed," she continued, "believe it or not she may have entered your life for a reason too. But face it, she got the job, you didn't. I think it's time that you accepted that. You know something, I read an article the other day online that reminded me of you. I printed it out. I was going to send it to you but I forgot. Let me get it. Hold on for a second, I have it here somewhere..."

A few minutes later.

"I'm back. Found it. Got it right here. Let me read it to you. The title of it is **'Avoid Just Ones'** and here's what it says:

*'Never rely on JUST ONE organization for your job security or to deliver your next promotion. No matter how good things seem where you are, things change in an instant. All it takes is JUST ONE person hired from the outside to take your job. Or JUST ONE unsupportive higher up or boss to*

*deny you a promotion.  Or JUST ONE reorganization to eliminate your job entirely and put you on the street.  No matter how secure you think you are in your current job, everyone needs a contingency plan or plan B.  Avoid JUST ONES in managing your career, they're limiting and unforgiving.'*

"That's it. Does this make any sense to you?"

"I'm not sure, mom. Are you suggesting that I quit my job?"

"Heavens no! Good jobs are too hard to find. And I know you've worked hard. But you can pursue your dreams anywhere. Your dad and I are proud of you, no matter what you do. You've already achieved more than we ever did. We just want you to be happy.  Life's too short to stay in a job you're miserable in. Are you happy, son?"

"Honestly…I don't know if I am or not."

"Then you should do something about it.  Now, I don't know what.  But don't do anything rash or stupid. Okay?"

"Don't worry I won't."

After sensing she had his full attention, she continued.

"Now as far as that woman is concerned, I don't know how you really feel about her, but from the tone in your voice when you talk about her, I can tell you really like her. That's just my intuition.  But why not cool it with her for now. Not forever, just until you sort things out.  You seem very confused right now."

"Thanks, mom. You always know the right things to say. Could you send me that article you read to me?"

"Sure. I'll scan it and email it to you right away."

They spoke for a little while longer before hanging up.

Not surprisingly, his mother had made him feel better about both his job, himself and Clare. And she definitely gave him some additional things to think about over the weekend.  If nothing else, she forced him to admit to himself that he wasn't totally happy, yet he had strong romantic feelings about Clare, and that deep down he wanted to see her succeed at Nu Foods.

He only wished she wasn't his boss.

# 22

## THE FIRST DAY

Monday arrived.

Both Clare and Drake got to the office early.

And they each planned to put last Friday's kiss behind them.

Clare was scheduled to spend the entire morning behind closed doors with Lois. Then she'd have lunch with Grisham. And then she'd spend the rest of the afternoon with the key members of the senior leadership team in one-on-one meetings, get updated by her administrative assistant and a couple of other members of her staff.

Her schedule was full. And as far as Drake was concerned, that was great.

He had a packed schedule too. Lots of client meetings and a couple of employee roundtables to keep him busy. And, as long as he could avoid running into her, everything was going to be fine. And if he kept saying that to himself over and over again, he might actually believe it. But try as he might, he kept day-dreaming about the way her lips had felt against his.

Nevertheless, five o'clock arrived quickly and he was feeling good.

This was an extremely productive day.

And he hadn't run into Clare.

But just as he was leaning back in his chair, she poked her head in his office.

"Mr. Williams, before you leave for the day. A word please. In my office."

She had her game face on, and he couldn't quite fathom what was going on under all that blonde hair of hers, which she had tied up in a bun. He followed her back to her office – and realized he was not going to end his day without seeing her.

When they arrived, he stood inside the doorway, like a naughty kid in the principal's office.

"Have a seat."

He slowly sat down.

She looked at him and got seated herself, but didn't say anything. The two of them stared at each other in silence for what seemed like an eternity.

Just before things were about to become awkward, she cleared her throat. "I've had a busy day. I just spent all morning with Lois, had a long lunch with Grisham and met some great people on the staff and on the senior leadership team. While Lois is gone, we have some HR priorities that I need your help with."

He was stunned.

She said nothing about what happened at the stump between them on Friday.

Instead this was...entirely and completely professional and businesslike.

Was she going to pretend that nothing happened?

"What do you have in mind, Clare?"

"There are a ton of things we need to do, but there are two things that are critical. First of all, we're going to need to step up our diversity and inclusion initiatives. I'd like your help in identifying some headhunters that specialize in finding diverse talent so that we can both screen them and put them to work. Grisham and I agree that half of our open manager positions over the next two years need to be filled with smart, diverse talent. Women. People of color. Free thinkers. Top universities. Renegades. Anybody different than what we have here now. We need to change this entire culture and bring in some hungry leaders with fresh innovative ideas to help us."

"Secondly," she continued, "we've got some bad managers here. I need your help in identifying who they are. And we need to put together an aggressive plan to either make them better or get rid of them. We need a welcoming culture for the all the new folks we'll be bringing in or the good people just won't stay. We need to send the message that it's not okay to treat people like crap – or let our managers get away with not giving their folks performance reviews, recognition or good feedback. In my mind, bad managers are guilty of managerial malpractice. If they can't or won't improve, we need to do what the medical profession does and pull their 'license' to manage anyone here ever again.

"Drake, I know all this isn't going to happen overnight, but it does need to happen. What do you think?"

"Wow. Those are some big time changes that are gonna piss a lot of people off. They will not be received well at all. It will take strong HR leadership to pull all this off."

"I know. I'm not naïve. But I'm prepared to take the heat. And Grisham's got my back on this too, which is crucial. Lois also believes these are exactly the things we need to do too. But I need your help. You know this company. I don't. I can't do this by myself. I'd like you to partner with me to help drive these changes. Okay?"

"Uh...alright. Whatever you say. You're the boss."

Not exactly enamored with this weak response, she glared at him coldly while remaining silent.

Taking that as a signal that their meeting was over, Drake took a chance and stood up.

She continued staring at him without uttering a word.

He then quietly left, impressed with how quickly she was getting down to business – serious business.

Even though she'd given him marching orders, he was going to do his damnedest to make sure the two of them were not alone at work again. He knew that realistically that was nearly impossible, even crazy.  But he wanted to avoid her as much as humanly possible.  It was too risky.

He didn't trust himself or his inner urgings.

Or hers for that matter.

He buried his head in his hands.

Why did everything have to be so hard?

What was going on with him?

And most importantly, why did he want to kiss her again?

# 23

## LOIS RETURNS

"Hi, Lois. I didn't know that you'd be back today. Wow, this last week has flown by so fast. Hey, give me a second and I'll get your desk all cleared off for you again."

Lois shook her head.

"Clare, don't bother. That desk is not mine anymore. It's yours now. I'm only here to help you for another week or so and then I'm officially off the payroll. Until I leave, I'll work from Joe's office in Sales. He's on vacation and I know he won't mind. So you stay right where you are, that's your chair now."

Lois sat down and made herself comfortable on the other side of the desk for once – and it felt good.

Clare was still just a little wary, but she slowly settled back in the chair. "So Lois, if you don't mind, can you tell me about that confidential project Grisham had you working on? Maybe I can help."

"Sure, of course. For the last week or so, I've been visiting a small juice company in North Carolina that Nu Foods is thinking about buying. Grisham asked me to visit them as part of the HR due diligence process. I confidentially met with the key leaders of that company and privately assessed their workforce capabilities. Grisham got me involved because you were new and he didn't want to distract you from getting up to speed here…especially when he's not even sure he wants to buy that company in the first place. Anyway, I'm writing up my final report now and I'll send it to both you and Grisham, since you'll have to follow up on it if Grisham decides to do the deal. Drake and Mike in benefits can help if you need them. And even though I'll be gone, feel free to hit me up with any questions. I'll make myself available. And don't worry, I won't charge you a dime."

They both laughed.

"Thanks Lois, I'll certainly take you up that offer. I really appreciate it."

"What have you been up to?" Lois asked.

Clare took a deep breath before describing her latest conversations with Grisham and her own innovative ideas for improving the company from an HR standpoint.

As she listened to Clare's ideas, she loved what she heard. Why hadn't she thought of some of these things herself? They would have added to her legacy before she left. Clare also talked about some of Drake's ideas too. She raved about how open and helpful he'd been in spearheading some key initiatives. Even though she didn't see him a lot, he saved her a lot of time by operating behind the scenes, helping her navigate through some of the office politics and personalities in the organization.

"Well, what do you think?" Clare's eyes were blazing with excitement, and her entire face was transformed as she waited eagerly for Lois' feedback.

Lois had to fight to keep her smile under wraps. "Your ideas are tremendous. I can see why Grisham is so excited about having you aboard. And..."

A long silence.

"What is it, Lois?"

"...I want to apologize to you. I'm so sorry for horrible way I treated you when we first met. I believe in loyalty and I was just being loyal to Drake. I was just trying to keep the promotion in house and reward him for all his hard work. He's a great guy, but I was wrong. You're exactly the kind of person this job needs."

"Thank you. That means a lot to me coming from you. I understand. Loyalty means a lot to me too. "

"Well, I mean it. You're terrific. And you know something else, I'm going to move up my last day. I don't need to be here much longer. You don't need me looking over your shoulder. You're on top of everything. And I'm a lame duck. I'm going to talk to Grisham about getting the heck out of here by end of the week."

# 24

## LOIS' LAST DAY

Friday was Lois' last day of work and it came quickly.

There was a farewell party for her in the Board Room. She made it clear to everyone she didn't want anything huge or expensive, even though she deserved it. Just something low key.

No one took her advice.

The Board Room was packed. And it overflowed with people outside of the room who couldn't even get in. Grisham presented her with a diamond necklace and delivered a great speech about her impact on the organization and the employees. Everyone on the leadership team spoke admiringly about her. Drake represented the HR team and talked glowingly about her mentoring to the team, her tough love and her strong leadership. Lois spoke last and did something no one else had ever recalled seeing her do in twenty-five years with the company.

She cried.

Afterwards, she slowly made the rounds to offer her personal goodbyes and give out hugs to folks individually.

She then made one last stop.

It was to Drake's office.

"Have a seat," he said.

When she did, she saw him staring at his laptop screen like he had no idea what to do with it.

"Mind if we talk for a minute before I head out for the last time."

"Sure," he said jerking his head up like he'd just been pulled out of a trance.

"Thank you for your kind words in the Board Room a few hours ago. I know after today, I'm officially not your boss anymore so I won't know if what I'm about to ask you to do will get done or not. But I do have one final request. I would like to ask you to be nice to Clare. I really like her. I think that she's the breath of fresh air that we've needed around here for a long time. And she absolutely raves about you.

"I think that the two of you will make an absolutely wonderful team that will make this company thrive far beyond Grisham's expectations. I've told her to call me if she has any problems or needs help. She's an amazing woman and I want to make sure that she's successful here. I know you're disappointed, but I hope that you'll decide to help her shine like you did with me."

"Thank you Lois, I will. I know you know how I feel about you. But let me say it again, you were an amazing boss. And I'll miss you."

He walked her out of the building, helping her load boxes of her personal belongings into her car. He then gave her a long hug.

When he returned to his desk, he shut down his laptop and looked forward to ending his day.

Just as he got up to leave, Clare walked in.

"Hey, I just wanted to see if you were okay. I know that you and Lois were very close. I bet you're really going to miss her, huh?"

"Yep, I will, definitely," he sighed. "Things won't be same here without her. She was one tough lady, but she really did a hell of a lot for me."

Then awkward silence.

And just before things got too uncomfortable, Clare spoke.

"Hey, I know that it's late on a Friday, but I'm still new and don't know anyone in Chicago. I was wondering if you might want to join me for a drink and perhaps I can tell you about some of the additional HR ideas Grisham and I have discussed. I'd love to get your thoughts about them."

She was giving him an expectant look and Drake could feel himself starting to sweat.

On the one hand, he had successfully dodged her for days and had tried to keep every conversation strictly business. But now, he couldn't stop thinking about the kiss that they'd shared at the stump. He didn't want a misstep that could cost him his job. Inside, his emotions were having an all-out brawl, and he had no idea what to do.

Meanwhile, she was looking at him with those eyes that seemed like they could see right through him, right down into his very soul.

Finally, he swallowed hard and nodded. "Uh...sure. I wouldn't mind at all."

"Great, I'll order us up a Uber and meet you downstairs."

# 25

## AFTER WORK

Clare had a perfect spot in mind.

In fact, as a newcomer to Chicago, she had been scouring the city and come across quite a few places she really liked. But for some reason, they weren't much fun without someone else to enjoy them with.

They both squeezed into a smaller-than-expected Toyota and she reminded the Uber driver to head to Arnie's in Lincoln Park.

During their ride, she chatted away about her week at work. As long as she kept the conversation about Nu Foods, he thought he'd be fine. However, he was already starting to feel his arm-pits sweat because he had a strange, uncomfortable feeling about this entire situation.

As the driver navigated the busy Chicago rush hour, he told himself over and over that he was going to regret this and that he wished he could muscle up the nerve to tell her that he'd changed his mind.

But, it was too late.

They turned off into a parking lot and the driver hit the brakes.

"This is it folks. We're here. Just so you know, that's fourteen bucks charged to your credit card, Ms. Hammond."

"Okay, sounds great. Thanks!" she said.

Drake, however, couldn't move, he wanted to tell her that he couldn't do this. He was taking a series of deep, calming breaths when she tapped him on the shoulder.

"Aren't you coming?"

Finally, he let out a big breath and nodded. "Uh...yep. Right behind you."

Maybe if he kept her talking, it would make the time go by faster, and then he could make up some excuse to get home. Yep, that sounded like a plan.

He followed behind her and when they walked in suddenly his mood changed instantly. It was one of those smooth jazz and piano bars where the lights were low and the atmosphere was soft and soothing. He had to admit that it was already putting him at ease.

He smiled and Clare caught it. "Hey, what is this place?"

"You sure you haven't been here before?" she asked accusingly.

"No. But I like it already. This is definitely my kind of joint."

"Good. I thought you'd like it."

He was fascinated by a man playing a white piano in a blue spotlight on the stage, and a woman dressed in bright red 1950's garb laying on top of it, crooning into a microphone.

The waiter came to lead them to a booth with an awesome view of the stage. Once the two of them settled in and ordered their drinks, she finally made a confession. "Okay, so I might have told a tiny little white lie to get you here. I don't really want to talk anymore about work. We can do that at the office."

He had been only half listening, but when she said that she'd basically lied to lure him here, she now had his full attention. He didn't know what to say, but before he could open his mouth to even ask why, she plunged ahead.

"I know that we're going to be working closely together and I want us to actually get to know each other better," she explained. "You've done a phenomenal job over the last few weeks. Even though we haven't seen a lot of each other, your emails and our brief conversations have helped me avoid making some potentially embarrassing rookie mistakes. Thank you. I don't want this to be another one of those typical boss-subordinate relationships. What I need is a true partner at work. Someone that I can really trust and collaborate with. So, I'd like to see if we can be friends. I think we can help each other."

He knew that she was marching into risky territory. But this place had him totally relaxed and alcohol was on its way over to him too. Right now, he couldn't figure out his priorities, much less keep them in the right order, and so he stopped struggling to be rational and decided to just deal with the moment.

"I'm okay with that," he agreed. "It'd be nice to have a friend at work. Lois and I had a great relationship for years. I considered her a partner, even though she was my boss and a hard ass. Deep down she had a heart of gold, was a great mentor and had only my best interests at heart. Besides her, I can't say that I have many work friends. To be honest, besides a couple of folks I can laugh and joke with, I don't have anyone at work I can really let my hair down with and confide in."

He was looking down at the table as he spoke and so he missed the look of sadness that flashed across her eyes.

She was actually hurting for him. "Drake, everyone deserves to have friends at work."

"I know," he responded finally looked up to meet her eyes. "I've given my heart and soul to that damn company. And in the process, I guess I've forgotten how to build real relationships."

There was bitterness and a bit of anger in his voice. Clare knew of course that he was directing it at himself, and not at her. And, she was elated that he was opening up to her and relieved they could finally talk candidly with each other, especially after the long week they both had just finished.

The waiter arrived with a tray holding their two drinks.

As they clicked their glasses together in a toast, she decided to change the topic, "I'm looking for a place to live. I'm tired of the Sheraton. But the prices of condos in this city are absolutely insane. Any recommendations?"

"Boy, I wish I could help out. I've lived in mine for three years and it's already gone up by fifty percent. So I know exactly what you mean. I was just lucky. But you'll find something."

"Damnit. It's all so depressing. I guess I'm just going to have to bite the bullet and pay a lot more for a place than I planned. Hey, can I tell you some crazy stories about the condos I've looked at so far?"

"Sure."

As she launched into her wacky condo hunting experiences, the waiter passed by and she caught his sleeve, ordering two more drinks for each of them.

One hour and many laughs later, they had both gotten gently buzzed. Suddenly, the song playing in the background changed and the bartender turned down the lighting even lower.

Most of their inhibitions had left them when they decided to go to the dance floor for a slow dance. As they held each other close and swayed to the music, Drake became transfixed on the singer who was now leaning up against the piano, but still crooning into the microphone as if she were romancing a lover instead singing to a bar full of strangers.

Clare, on the other hand, pressed her head on his shoulder and her mind raced to the kiss that they'd shared at the stump. She had wanted to bring that up and talk about it all evening, but didn't have the nerve.

When the music stopped, they both decided it was time to call it a night.

It surprised both of them when he insisted on sharing a ride with her to drop her off at her hotel. He stressed that at ten o'clock at night, an attractive female riding alone in Chicago was risky. Especially a woman who was now clearly drunk. He wanted to make sure nothing happened and that she got back to her hotel safely.

When they arrived at the Sheraton, this time he covered the Uber fare and then helped her out and onto her feet.

She giggled while he steadied her and told him that she might have to lean on him since her heels made it more difficult than usual to walk. He chuckled and told her it was fine. He mentioned he'd left his own high heels at home, so he understood. This only made her laugh so hard that she had to wipe tears from her eyes.

When they reached the entrance to her room, she reached into her purse and found her electronic room key. She fiddled with it a bit and then finally opened the door. But she hesitated before going in like she wanted to say something to him. He, on the other hand, wanted to kiss her again and badly, but he wasn't sure if it was such a good idea.

Besides, he knew she was intoxicated and shouldn't take advantage of her, but he couldn't resist. What was the harm in one short friendly goodbye kiss? He braced himself, then put his hand under her chin and tilted it down and placed a light kiss on her forehead.

Just like the first time, she was frozen for a few seconds, not sure what was happening, but then lifted her head up and she kissed him back right on the lips. He was ready to disengage from her and go home. But then he found that her hands were on the back of his head, pushing his lips even more firmly against hers. And he could feel her soft, supple body pressed against his. It was so tight he had to loosen his collar to give himself some breathing room. Then she whispered for him to come inside and he gave in.

Once she closed the door behind the two of them, she stopped for a second, unsure of what to do next. Drake came up to her again, kissed her and she sprung back to life.

She deepened the kiss, and the two of them began to shed their clothes. Eventually, he walked her backwards to the bed, gently pushed her back on it and followed her.

He was nervous, because she was opening up parts of him that he'd kept buried for a long, long time, and he was afraid of what might emerge.

He didn't have to wait too long.

The two of them made love, practically all night.

When they were finished, she curled up his arms. And the two of them slept peacefully until late the next morning, both of them thinking about each other -- but wondering where this night might be leading them.

# 26

## THE DAY AFTER

DRAKE WOKE UP FIRST the next day in her hotel room. And his head was pounding. Not because of the alcohol, but with the vivid memories of the night before. He was still lying flat on his back, with Clare lying naked in his arms, softly sleeping. As he opened his eyes and saw her soft skin beneath him, he nibbled his way from her earlobe down to her mouth.

She had opened up that forbidden door he feared.

And as much as he wanted to walk through it, hand in hand with her, he knew that she was still his boss. And if the kiss by the stump could make things awkward at work between them, what the hell was last night going to do?

As he lay there trying to sort out his thoughts and feelings, he kept getting aroused by how good she'd felt, and how her body seemed to be a perfect fit with his. He'd gone to heights last night that he hadn't felt in a long time. His body was responding, even now, just to the mere thought of what they'd done with each other last night.

He put his free hand over his face and groaned. It was an anguished sound, and though it wasn't loud, it instantly woke her up. Her blue eyes fluttered open and she raised her head from his shoulder.

With both of them now awake, she sat up and pulled the sheets up to her chin with her face beet red.

"I guess good morning would be the wrong thing to say right about now, wouldn't it?" She'd clearly meant it as a joke, but he didn't find it funny.

He was angry, not at her, but at himself. He could have stopped all of this before it even started, and now it was his fault that he hadn't. He put his head in his hands, "I'm so sorry, Clare. Last night shouldn't have happened."

His face was still buried in his hands, so he didn't see the hurt frown that crossed her face. "This got totally out of control. I didn't want you riding back here by yourself last night, given all the muggings happening lately. And then, I couldn't help myself when I kissed you. I never thought in a million years it would wind up like this. I let things go waaaay too far and I'm so sorry. This is all my fault."

He still hadn't looked up at her. And she was beginning to understand that he was hiding his eyes because he didn't want to face her.

"What the hell makes you think you're the only one responsible for last night?" Her anger gave an edge to her voice that instantly grabbed his attention. Her expression was stormy and her once blue eyes were now a slate gray he knew was not a good sign.

He repeated, "I just don't want you to feel like I slept with you as payback or just to keep my job. Because I didn't! Look, after working with you all these weeks, I think you're great. You really deserved Lois' job. There, I said it!"

Her hands were knotted in the sheets so angrily that she could have ripped them apart if she wanted to. "What the hell is up with you? Is work all you care about? Don't you feel like there's a little bit more between us than just work? Tell me right now, because I need to know the truth before I make any other decisions."

Her eyes flashed angrily at him and he understood that it was now a warning, and a test. He just didn't know what he had to say in order to pass. He fell silent for a few moments, then slid out of her bed and began to get dressed -- turning his back to her as he put on his socks.

This just angered her further, making her feel like she was just a cheap one night stand. Responding in kind, she wrapped the bedsheet around her body, turned her back to him and stalked off to the bathroom to start the water for a shower.

When she came out, she saw a fully dressed Drake making his way over to the door of her room. As he opened it, he said, "Clare, I really had a great time last night. I'm just a little confused right now. See you Monday."

And with that, he closed the door quietly and left.

She walked over to lock the door and then slammed the bed pillows to the floor in frustration. She couldn't shake her anger. He needed to make up his damn mind about what they were to each other and that list of options didn't include her being just a one-time, booty-call.

Going into the bathroom, she stepped into the water already running in the shower. It almost felt like the water was angry, too. It was hot, which matched her mood. She gasped at first, as the first spray of water scalded her, but she adjusted to it and decided to keep it hot.

She wanted to wash off the smell of a guy she really liked at first -- a man she now really cared for -- along with memories of their glorious night together. She wanted it all rinsed off her body, down the drain into the sewer where it belonged.

Or did she?

# 27

## A NEW BEGINNING

That weekend, Drake was in his own personal dream world. Everything felt surreal and his mind was in a fog.

When Monday came, he didn't feel like going to the stump and possibly running into Clare. He couldn't sleep so he decided to head out early for work. A few minutes after he arrived at his desk, his phone rang. Damnit, he thought, it's six-thirty in the goddamn morning, nobody's here, who the hell could be calling me now.

He looked down at the phone, didn't recognize the number and thought about not answering it. But he couldn't do that. It could be a client emergency or something urgent.

"Hello, this is Drake Williams."

"Drake, I'm Robert Cunningham. Sorry to call you so early. I'm with Kingston Executive Search. Let me get to the point. We have a client, a U.S. based technology firm, looking to expand globally who is looking for a Vice President of Human Resources. This job is located in downtown Chicago, but has small growing divisions all around the country. You interested?"

He never got contacted by headhunters anymore, primarily because he stopped returning their calls. This time however felt different. "Hi, Robert. Appreciate the call. Would you mind telling me how you got my name in the first place?"

"Uh…unfortunately, Drake I can't. Usually, I do. But in this case, the person who has referred you is a close friend of mine. Highly credible. But prefers to remain anonymous at this time. I can tell you they recommend you highly. And based on what they've described, you seem to have all HR skills and experience we're looking for."

Collecting himself, he said: "I appreciate that, Robert. But I'm not looking. I'm happy here. I haven't even thought about leaving my organization. Besides my resume isn't up to date and my LinkedIn profile is woefully out of whack. And--"

Robert interrupted: "I know. I already looked you up on LinkedIn and your profile definitely needs a lot of work. That's not a problem. We can deal with that and your resume too. But I don't want to waste your time or mine, if you're not at least interested in hearing more about the job."

Thinking for a few more seconds, he responded. "Okay, that's fair. Tell me more?"

Robert described the opportunity, the compensation range, the culture, business strategy and the CEO in detail. He also described what they were looking for in their new HR VP.

Wow! Drake thought to himself, the job description fit him like a glove. "Robert, that all sounds intriguing. What would be the next step?"

"Tell you what Drake, I'm located near you. I want to move fast on this. The company needs someone yesterday. Why don't we meet at the Starbucks a few blocks from your office at Dearborn and Lake? Frankly, my client is very picky and I need to size you up in person before presenting you to them. My reputation is on the line here. If that works for you, let's meet in an hour."

"Great, no problem Robert. See you there."

As Drake loaded up his laptop shoulder bag and prepared to leave, he racked his brain trying to figure who could have possibly referred him. His contact network was almost non-existent. He had alienated all of his college buddies or anyone that could talk him up for other jobs. He hadn't been active in the Chicago HR association or any other networking groups in years. And it had been almost forever since he interviewed for any job outside of Nu Foods.

But he couldn't worry about any of that that now. He didn't have a lot of time to walk over to this meeting.

When he arrived, he was greeted by short, stocky man in a gray business suit.

"Hi, are you Drake?"

"Yes, great to meet you Robert."

And with that they ordered their coffees at the counter, found a private corner and got down to business.

Drake, on his walk over, had gotten himself mentally prepared. He replayed in his mind all the mistakes Lois said he made interviewing a few weeks ago with Grisham and the senior team. He was now grateful for her direct, un-sugarcoated feedback and was not going to repeat those same screw ups now.

And he didn't.

With Robert, he was confident, poised and kept his answers punchy, positive and upbeat. He even displayed some subtle humor and smiled, which made Robert laugh, which was unusual given his serious nature. They had an enjoyable discussion. Maybe his mom had been right. Maybe everything did happen for a reason. This was a terrific opportunity and potentially a big career break. He could feel it. The more they talked, the more he hungered to find out more about this job. Because the company was based right downtown where he was, he wouldn't even have to move. That was an added plus.

Finally Robert wrapped things up. "Drake, I think you're an excellent fit for my client," he said. "Let's move quickly on this. Can you take a few days off this week for interviews?"

"Sure."

"Terrific. Let me give you some things."

Robert then reached into his black shoulder bag. "Here are their last two annual reports. Here's a detailed description of the job. And here's a stack of public documents about the company's short and long term business strategy. This is homework! You should cram like you're taking a final exam and make sure you know this stuff like you've been with their company ten years. I know this is all on short notice. But if you're still interested, and can fit in some time to study this stuff, I'll call the client, set up the interview schedules and talk to you tonight. You in?"

"Sounds great. I'm in. I'm going to call my boss and take the rest of the day off to review all these materials and do my own online research on the company. One other thing, can you send me bios on all the people I'll be interviewing?"

"Absolutely. You'll have those tonight. You should check them out on LinkedIn too?"

"Will do."

Drake did his best not to openly sound like he was over-eager for this opportunity, but he was bursting with enthusiasm inside. But knew he had a lot of work to do. He wanted to nail this interview, dazzle these people and at least get the offer. Then he'd decide what to do from there.

That evening, Robert emailed and phoned him with everything he promised. Drake would need to take Tuesday, Wednesday and Thursday off and would return back to work on Friday. His interview schedule would include meetings in Chicago and day trips to Dallas and New York to meet key leaders in their Southwest and East Coast operations as well.

He was pumped.

Was this potentially the start of a new beginning?

He would quickly find out.

# 28

## VACATION DAYS

After Drake left her hotel room, Clare spent that entire weekend lying in bed. She didn't know what to think about the Friday night she'd spent with Drake. On Saturday and Sunday, she never left her room, ordering room service all weekend for her meals.

Occasionally, she'd click on the TV. But after a few minutes she'd quickly flip it off preferring instead to be alone with her thoughts.

She took turns staring at the ceiling.

And being listless and depressed.

She dozed off and on, all weekend in an endless cycle. And before she knew it Monday morning arrived and she woke up tired, not knowing what to do or feel about Drake.

She arrived at work late on Monday and didn't see Drake in his office.

Later that morning, she picked up his voicemail: *"Clare, something's come up. I'm going to need to take a few vacation days. I'll email the diversity turnover report you asked for and the employee engagement numbers for the Operations group I promised you later today. That way, you'll have them for your meeting with Grisham tomorrow. I've asked Sydney, the new*

*HR manager on my team to be your contact while I'm out. She's new, but she's crunched all the numbers in those two reports and knows them better than I do. Feel free to leave me any other messages and I'll get back to you right away. Take care."*

His message took her by surprise.

But much to her amazement, without Drake around, her day ran smoothly and seemingly on autopilot. Nevertheless, she found herself missing him. She was definitely on an emotional roller coaster about their encounter. Though it felt good then, it didn't feel so good now. But she'd have to wait until he returned to sort everything out.

The next morning when she arrived and got off the elevator, she went straight to Drake's desk to see if he'd gotten back. She checked in with Sydney every couple of hours to find out if she'd heard anything from Drake.

No word.

She did this every day until Friday, when he finally returned.

Peeking in his office, she saw him seated with his back turned and was elated. Preparing herself for the worst, she knocked on his closed door. His deep voice invited her in. He was poring over a letter and didn't look up right away as she entered.

"I see you're back from vacation," she said cautiously.

"Um, yes. I was getting some things in order. Sorry I didn't give you more notice ahead of time. It was kind of a spur of the moment thing. Hopefully, Sydney was able to help you out while I was gone."

"Yep, Sydney was awesome. She's a real talent. We're definitely going to have to figure out how to use her even more. But tell me, what's up? Is it your mom and dad? Are they okay?" she probed.

"Thanks for asking. Nah, nothing wrong with them. They're both great. Probably in better shape than I am and still dropping hints about me giving 'em grandkids. So they're cool," he chuckled.

"Whew, that's a big relief, I didn't know what to think," she responded seriously. "But you were out almost all week, is there anything I should know about, Drake?"

110

She was hoping that this would subtly shift the topic back to the night they spent together.

Drake nervously stroked his chin for a few uncomfortable moments. Finally, he turned around and picked up that letter that he'd been staring at so closely on his desk and handed it to her.

"Here. This is for you."

She was confused as she looked at him for a second or two, before lowering her eyes to the document. She read it to herself three or four times, but she just couldn't make herself believe what it said. No, it just couldn't be true. Things were working out so great between them on the job.

Now this?

IT WAS HIS LETTER OF RESIGNATION.

"What's this? Don't you think that you owe me more of an explanation instead of just shoving this note in my hand?"

There was anger in her voice, and hurt, but most of all, shock. She couldn't believe it. Was he really so upset at her that he was just going to up and leave?

"Clare, it's my two weeks' notice. For the last three days, I've been out interviewing with Green Crest Technologies here in the city."

"So, all of a sudden you went to an interview," she said, still in shock. "You could have at least told me Friday night at the bar when we were together."

"I would have. But I didn't know about it then. It happened out of the blue on Monday. I got an early morning call from a headhunter who talked to me about the HR VP job at Green Crest. It sounded fantastic. So, I went to the interview and they offered me the job two days ago."

His voice had no emotion because he didn't want to add any more fuel to the fire than he'd already done by handing her his notice.

"And of course you accepted it."

It wasn't a question.

It was clear he'd accepted it.

Drake looked at her, trying to figure out what he was supposed to say. He simply nodded, then winced, as if he was expecting her to hit him or yell at him for daring to leave the company when they still had so much work to do.

"Yes, Clare, I did accept the job. However, I felt I owed you the courtesy of a two weeks' notice, unless you want to kick me out now. Look, I don't want to leave you high and dry. And I know the timing isn't great. But I promise I'll work my tail off to help you until I leave. Let me do that for you."

"I appreciate that Drake," she said clearly disappointed. "But if you think that's supposed to be a consolation prize for me, you're wrong. Where the hell am I supposed to get someone who knows Nu Foods as well as you do in two weeks?"

Clearly, she was doing her best to keep her temper in check. But she was pissed and couldn't believe that he would just up and quit on her with no forewarning.

What was she going to do?

# 29

## THE FINAL WEEKS

The next two weeks were a blur.

Drake wanted to leave Nu Foods on good terms. And so he threw himself into everything Clare delegated to him. He did this while finishing up his own work and while also training the new HR manager, Sydney, who would soon be promoted.

He felt remorseful about quitting so suddenly and wanted to make up for the roller coaster ride he'd taken her on over the last few weeks. He wanted to give her the same commitment and support he had given Lois. So he started skipping his early morning workouts at the stump. Instead, he started coming into the office even earlier than normal, this time six in the morning and leaving at eight in the evening.

But that wasn't all.

He gave Clare his best advice.

He talked her up positively to everyone in the organization.

The only thing he avoided was one-on-ones with her. He didn't trust himself. It wasn't that he still hated her for taking away the job that he'd wanted so desperately. Now it was because he could finally admit to himself that he had fallen deeply in love with her and didn't trust himself -- or his emotions -- if they were alone by themselves.

But, meanwhile, she was clearly still angry. He could tell because despite all the help he was providing her, when they were in meetings, she'd take subtle little digs at him in front of others. And it hurt.

Often, she'd even approach him to pick arguments over tiny things just to create conflict between them. Each clash they had seemed to cut deep. And before the wounds had time to heal, there'd be another one, slicing down even further until it reached his heart. Clearly, it seemed she wanted to get back at him for not only leaving, but for all the times he'd been a jerk.

AND IN HIS MIND, SHE WAS ABSOLUTELY RIGHT.

He had treated her badly.

He ruthlessly lied to her about Lois.

Whenever she had revealed her true feelings and made herself personally vulnerable, he had returned the favor by walking away from her with no explanation.

In addition to all this, she had gone out of her way to support him at Nu Foods, gave him great career advice, connected him with important people in her network and had demonstrated on numerous occasions that she was solidly in his corner.

In return, he'd been an utterly insensitive asshole and was now running off, leaving her high and dry.

So, yes, in his mind, she was totally justified in extracting her pound of flesh from him now.

But, this time, he had no urge to strike back.

He didn't want to fight anymore.

He knew he had no one to blame but himself for the state of their relationship. Or rather, their non-relationship. Sure, she'd beaten him out for the job at Nu Foods. But she was clearly the better candidate. And he'd told her that. He had finally come to terms with it. And he was now ready to move on.

All he wanted to do was support her in his final weeks and leave the organization with grace.

However, as he was winding down his tenure, he was discovering a bright side to all this.

With no career at Nu Foods to be concerned about anymore, he began focusing more on observing Clare. He paid particular attention to her leadership, humor and the engaging manner she displayed often with the employees and leaders of the organization -- and how they responded in much the same manner. Subtly, he found himself mimicking some of her interactions with people in his final days at the company. And, it was remarkable how much more positively people responded to him as a result. He began picking up on little things he never knew or cared to about before, and they were all fascinating. As a result, he began seeing his colleagues and himself in a new light.

All he could think about was how all this was coming at the perfect time. These were all lessons he could take with him to Green Crest and give him a fresh start. **In his new job, he was going to make sure to spend more time building relationships – both inside and outside of the organization -- and taking time for himself versus being a workaholic who never knew when to quit.** He had Clare to thank for that and he planned to tell her all this before he left.

But not now.

She was still too pissed.

Being alone with her was still a dangerous proposition.

And so he continued to count down the days until the torture would end.

And it would come soon enough.

# 30

## THE LAST DAY

DRAKE'S LAST DAY at Nu Foods finally arrived.

Earlier that day, he had his own farewell party in the Board Room.

No diamond necklace though.

But nevertheless, the room was packed, lots of well-wishes from colleagues and glowing farewell comments from both Grisham and from Clare.

Afterwards, the rest of his day went by fast.

When 6 p.m. rolled around he stayed to say his final good-byes to the incoming evening security staff that had helped him a lot over the years. To his surprise, they pitched in and gave him an envelope with an Amazon gift card as their going away gift.

Touched and filled with emotion, he hugged them all and left to go back upstairs for the final time.

Back at his office, he ran his hand over the arm rest of his chair then over the smooth surface of his desk. He'd spent a lot of time here instead of with his parents, dating or with his old buddies from back home. And in a way, he was now breaking the grip that this job had held over him all these years.

He left the key to his desk in the top drawer. And would give his key card to the security folks on his way out.

He made his way to the elevator. When he pushed the down arrow, he had to wait a few minutes. He could see that the elevator was a few floors above him, but had stopped.

It now hit him: the time for a new chapter was now upon him.

The elevator finally came to a stop on his floor with a metallic ding, then the doors slid open...*to reveal Clare!*

Drake felt like his heart stopped.

"You still here?" she said, clearly surprised to see him. "I thought you would have gone home by now."

"I'm leaving now and--"

"Well, I've just come down from Grisham's office. Would you mind holding the elevator for me until I go get my things? I'm leaving now too."

Her voice had no inflection in it, and so he had no idea what she was thinking or feeling.

For the last few weeks, it was rare they were alone together. And now he was going to be in a small elevator space with her for a span of thirty seconds in which there would be no witnesses and where they could get into another argument.

He didn't want that. So he turned around and slowly began to walk away. "Yes, but I...uh...I forgot something back at my desk. Then I need to stop by the men's room. Why don't you go ahead on down?"

"What? I know what you're doing. You've been avoiding me. You just don't want to be alone with me in that elevator. Don't lie to me. Tell the truth, Drake."

Stunned by her bluntness, he stopped dead in his tracks and turned around. Then he sighed heavily and dragged his eyes up to meet hers. "Yeah...okay...you're right. Look, I just don't want to get into it with you anymore. Anytime we're by ourselves all we do is fuss and fight, and I'm all worn down."

She was silent, but he could tell she hadn't expected him to say that.

Her face softened.

"Then let's not fight on your last elevator ride down to the lobby. Okay?"

117

Whether or not she actually meant it, he wasn't sure. But he bit his lip and decided to give in, waiting by the elevator until she picked up her purse and shoulder bag.

They then got in the elevator together.

Their ride began in silence, before she spoke up.

"You know something, I really wish you weren't leaving."

"Well, you have a strange way of showing it. Honestly, sometimes it seemed like you were pushing me out."

"Sorry about that. Sometimes when I'm angry, I hold a grudge too long. That's one of many things about myself I hate. But the truth is you've really helped me out a lot over the last few weeks and I really appreciate it."

"Thanks."

"I know you're going to do a great job at Green Crest."

The very slow elevator moved down another floor or two.

"Clare, you're going to do great here too. I know I've said this before. But I'll say it again. You're perfect for this job. I've been very impressed watching you operate in the last few weeks. Despite all the grief you've given me lately, I know you're a wonderful person down deep."

There, they were being nice to each other. See? They could get along if they wanted to. The slow elevator had five more floors to go before they would be getting out to say their final goodbyes.

On a whim, at the same time, both of them turned towards each other with their mouths open as if to say something. Yet both of them couldn't get the words out. So they stood there in silence, just looking at each other.

One second passed, then another, and by the third, they were kissing. Their arms were wrapped around each other tightly, and all the feelings the two of them had tried to bottle up for the last few weeks had found a way to burst to the surface, culminating in one large explosion of romantic passion.

And one final kiss…goodbye.

Or was it?

As the elevator doors opened, they each pulled away from each other.

But they still stared into each other's eyes as they did so.

Neither of them left the elevator.

"Listen Clare, I don't work here anymore. Would you mind coming over to my condo for a drink?"

"Sounds great. Let's go."

# 31

## LATER AT DRAKE'S PLACE

"Clare, I'm sure that you'll find someone to replace me. I know everyone's not a workaholic like me, but that may be a good thing for you. You just promoted Sydney and she's going to help a lot."

She didn't want to talk about Sydney or work for that matter. And so she drained her glass of wine and kissed him. He didn't resist. As their clothes fell to the floor, they moved off of his cramped couch down to his soft carpet. One thing was leading to another, and the next thing that Drake knew, he was feeling everything that he'd felt in their previous encounter weeks ago.

That was when Clare ruined the moment.

"Drake, did you really have to quit now? We could have made this work. It would have been great if you could have waited six months. Everything seemed to be going so good."

Drake didn't want to argue with her, but there were certain things that touched a nerve, and this was one of them. He was not going to just sit back and let this go.

"Six months? That's forever! The Green Crest job would have been filled in six months. Look, I worked my tail off for that job, just like you did for the one at Nu Foods. Why should I have had to put my career on hold just to help you out? Don't you think you're being just a little bit selfish?"

"Maybe. But I'm sure I could have convinced Grisham to make you HR VP of that new juice company that we've decided to buy. That way, you wouldn't have to move and you'd be the top dog in HR for that company and still be part of our Nu Foods team here in Chicago."

"But I'd still be reporting to you, wouldn't I?"

"Yes, but--"

"Then I really would NOT be the top dog, would I? No offense, but it's time for me to step out on my own. And it's too late anyway. I start the new job on Monday."

"I know, but..."

The two of them continued arguing on this point back and forth until they were both exhausted. And then they sat in angry silence on the floor for a few minutes, still undressed. Would their jobs always get in the way?

Finally, Clare spoke up: "Look, I apologize. What I said was absolutely stupid. You're right, I was being selfish and looking out for me, not you. Sometimes I am too argumentative for my own good. That's the competitive swimmer in me that just wants to win all the time. I need to stop doing that. I don't need to come out on top all the time... I just want you."

And with that, they embraced, pushed their clothes aside and continued on the carpet where they had left off.

That morning, Clare woke up first. "You know something, I was just thinking about what we talked about last night."

"Hey, I thought we agreed that you wouldn't--"

"No, this is entirely different. Hear me out. This is a good thing. What you said hit home. The part where you said I was being selfish."

"Now, Clare--"

"Wait a minute, Drake, let me finish. I don't want to be selfish anymore with you. In fact, I want to help you get off to a great start at Green Crest. Just like you did for me these last few weeks. Please hear me out."

"Okay. Alright."

"Awesome. First off, I agree with you. Since you're leaving, it's time to put Nu Foods in the rear view mirror and begin looking forward and thinking longer-term. It's time for you to take total control over your career."

"I couldn't agree more. That's what I wanted to say last night before things got heated. But how do I do that? What's your angle?"

"Well, there's an exercise I did when I got divorced."

"Oh yeah, what was that?"

"When my marriage broke up, I took some time to come up with a list of *guiding principles for managing my life.* A marriage counselor mentor of mine recommended that I do that before my divorce was finalized. **He told me that the best way of rebounding from a setback was to develop some personal guidelines for moving forward in the future so that you don't make the same mistake again.** And it really worked. It was the best thing I ever did. In fact, I was attracted to you because you met many of the principles on my list."

"Well, I'm certainly grateful for that," he said. "And I'm happy it helped you get through your divorce too. But do you really think that applies to me and my new job?"

"Yep, I do. I think the same approach will work. Developing the right guiding principles – and following them – can help you avoid making the same mistakes all over again. They can help ensure you don't get overlooked for those promotions in the future you deserve. Or at least allow you to recognize great opportunities you're not aware of when you see them. That's what I think they can do for you. **So what do you think about developing some *guiding principles for managing your career?*"**

"Hmm…I don't know. Maybe you're on to something. Or maybe not. But at this point, I'm willing to give just about anything a try. And I could definitely use some help as I start this new gig. But I don't have a clue how to begin even doing something like this?"

**"I do. Here's my idea. I know some absolutely fantastic people in my network that have done well in their careers.**

**Some are executives running large organizations. Some are consultants and awesome HR leaders. All of them have had big disappointments in their careers.** Some have had failures so painful you wouldn't believe. **But all of them are phenomenally successful today. They'll give you some great pointers for navigating your career. Talk to them. Listen to what they have to say. You don't have to buy everything they say. Just take from them only what you need. Ignore the rest. Tap into them to come up with your own set of career guiding principles.** What do you think? Would you be at least willing to give it try?"

"Sure. I trust your judgment on stuff like this. And frankly, I could use some good advice as I start this new job. I've been going it alone for so long."

"Great. I'll connect you with some of my people."

"That would be awesome. Like you, sometimes my ego gets in my way too. **Getting some guidance from those who've traveled the road I'm now on would be fantastic.** Like you said, I don't want to repeat the same mistakes I've made before."

"Sounds good. Give me a few days. I'll make some calls and start hooking you up."

"Thanks, Clare. I'm excited. I'm really looking forward to this."

They were looking at each other now, and the anger from last night had completely melted away from both of their faces. The look on his face told her that there was something he wanted to say, but was hesitating.

"What's wrong?" she said. "I know you well enough by now to know that there's something on your mind and you're trying to think of the best way to say it. Just spit it out."

"I love you, Clare." The words just burst forth, without warning, and hit her with an emotional force she didn't expect. She could actually feel her eyes widening at his admission.

"I don't know a more delicate way of putting it," he continued. "So I'm sorry if you wanted to hear it in a more romantic way. But I can only tell you what I feel in my heart right now. I can't believe with everything I've put you through, that you're willing to extend yourself to help me out like this. I love that about you. And I love you."

She frowned...and then smiled.

He looked up at her as if he expected her to rip his heart out.

Not this time.

"I love you, too, Drake," she confessed. "To be honest, I was just physically attracted to you at first. But you took my heart when we talked on that stump that second time. But then you confused me. One day you were nice to me and then another day you'd blow me off. When you decided to resign, it really hurt me bad and had me confused too. But that's when I knew I really cared about you. I'm so, so sorry I've been taking it out on you for the last few weeks. Anyone else who was leaving would have sabotaged me or let me sink on my own. You didn't. You took all my bullshit. And you were there for me. Supporting me. Talking me up to everyone in the company. That's the Drake I've fallen in love with."

The two of them talked, late into the afternoon, without arguing for once, and Clare decided to stay the night there with him.

As it turned out, they had all their meals delivered, and she never left his condo the entire weekend.

It was the best and most pleasurable three days either of them had ever had.

# 32

## SIX MONTHS LATER...

Things were going great for Clare at Nu Foods. Grisham and the leadership team were thrilled with her performance and the company's financial results.

The HR changes she was spearheading were challenging, but being received positively. Company-wide diversity and inclusion results were slowly improving. Innovation at the company was on the upswing. And her leadership of the HR team was tremendous. There was still a lot more work that needed to be done, but she was off to a fantastic start.

SHE HAD ALSO BEEN KEEPING IN TOUCH WITH LOIS via email and text. With Drake gone, Clare found herself leaning on Lois even more than she planned. And now regarded her as one of her closest friends and mentors.

They had formed a great bond over the past few months, even though they rarely saw each other in person. Every few days, she would call or text Lois for some advice on navigating a sticky political situation or a problem personality at Nu Foods. They had quite a few late night calls. And she'd been using Lois as a sounding board on her ideas before running them by Grisham and the leadership team. Her predecessor proved to be a wise and savvy advisor and collaborator.

And Clare couldn't wait to touch base with her in person and was thrilled that she had accepted her invitation to meet for dinner to chat. It was an opportunity for both women to catch up on all the changes that were going on in their respective lives.

When they met, they laughed and talked at length about the blast Lois was having in retirement and all the exotic travel she and Thomas were doing.

They then switched topics, "How's Drake doing?"

Clare smiled. "He's really doing fantastic at Green Crest. He's in great spirits these days. He loves it so much, and he comes home every night and tells me about it."

"Home? Are you guys living together now?"

"Yep, we are. To be honest, it was a surprise. But he got tired of me complaining about Chicago condo prices and asked me to move in with him about six weeks ago. It wasn't exactly what I planned when I came here. But it's much better than I imagined. I just love living in the city and being with him makes me feel alive in so many ways."

"Now that you're both together, give me the real scoop on how you guys met," Lois asked. "I just know bits and pieces."

"Well, the part you know already is that I met Drake accidentally at the lake before my interview. But when I joined the company, our relationship began to slowly blossom. However, neither of us wanted to recognize it. So we had plenty of ups and downs. But when he decided to leave the company, that's really when we found each other. And we've been together ever since. Now, every morning, he and I get up and run the same path that he had run for years by himself. To our special spot. A stump by the lake. He then stops and does his exercises and meditates, while I take a quick dip in the water. Sometimes, if no one's around, we might share a few quick smooches. It was how we met months ago. It's amazing, when we get there, we both feel so invigorated. It's like nothing in the world can hold us back. We love each other have a fantastic relationship."

"That's great. I'm so happy for both of you guys."

"Thanks. The only thing we can't figure out yet is how he got that job so soon after I started. He wasn't looking for anything. His network was dead. And he allowed all of his business relationships outside of the company to dry up. He and I still talk about how this headhunter called him completely out of the blue with the ideal HR job. Pure fate, I guess."

Lois looked around the restaurant, as if she expected someone to be eavesdropping on them, then leaned in closer to Clare before she spoke.

"Call me Fate. That's my new name: Fate. It was me."

"You!"

"Yes, me. I confess. In my last week with the company, I could see how miserable he was and I called one of my own mentors, actually the CEO of Green Crest, who is Drake's boss now. When that CEO heard I retired, he asked me to come work for him as his head of HR. When I told him I'd retired for good, I recommended Drake. And so he used his company's search firm to reach out to him just as a favor to me. And when Drake went in, I think he felt like he had nothing to lose. Anyway, he just blew everyone away!"

She smiled sheepishly at Clare, who was caught somewhere between a thankful smile and a shocked expression.

Lois continued, "I must say, both of you tried to hide your feelings for one another. And I commend you guys for staying professional on the job. But it was obvious to me from day one that there was romantic tension and sparks between the two of you, no matter how much you tried to hide it. I may be getting old, but I'm not blind yet."

She winked at Clare, who couldn't help but burst out laughing. "Was it really that obvious?"

"Duh! Yeah. Painfully obvious. Now admit it, neither one of you would have comfortable if you were still his boss. Am I right or am I right?"

Clare gave an embarrassed nod. She knew that was true.

Lois went on, "And I couldn't very well tell him that I was the one responsible for getting him the interview at his new company, could I? You know Drake. He has entirely too much pride. He'd consider it some kind of handout. He wants to make it on his own. **But I don't think he really understood**

**how the game is played in large organizations -- you scratch my back and I'll scratch yours. And he scratched my back a lot over the years. And returning the favor was the least I could do."**

She continued: "I knew that Drake would impress the hell out of my old mentor. And the rest is history." And with that, Lois leaned back in her seat now that her secret had been revealed.

"Well, I for one am very thankful to you," Clare said. "I know Drake would be too and--"

Lois instantly flung her hands up to cut off Clare's sentence.

"Hey, I really don't think that he needs to know that right now. If he's happy about it, let's not ruin it for him, okay? Maybe after a few more weeks. But not now. Deal?"

"Okay. Deal. But I do have to tell him, but I promise you I'll find the right moment to let him know."

"I understand. Thanks. I know you'll handle it delicately. I just don't want him to be angry with me, considering that I failed him," Lois said as she looked down sadly into her glass of wine.

Reading her disappointment, Clare put her hand on Lois' and squeezed it.

"How on earth could you possibly have failed him?" Clare was confused.

"I could have prepared him better for future opportunities. Don't get me wrong, YOU were the best person to take my job, because of all the extensive relationships you'd built, your strong leadership, your engaging personality and the HR experiences you had working in various companies. That's what really lost it for Drake. The leadership committee picked you because of all those things."

It was all now coming out.

"But he's happy now, so all's well that ends well, right?" Clare said brightly as their food arrived.

Lois looked down at her plate but didn't touch her silverware. "No it isn't. He needed more from me as his boss and mentor. **Perhaps I should have encouraged him to do more networking and relationship building. Perhaps even encouraged him**

**to leave the company sooner to pick up the critical experiences he needed.** Another thing I should have done is--"

"Lois, stop. You did a lot. Drake told me about the brutally candid feedback you gave him after his interview with Grisham and the leadership team. He said you were pretty rough on him."

"Yeah, he's right. I admit I was pretty harsh. And maybe a little pissed off too. Was he angry at me about that? Be honest. I could tell that it didn't go over too well."

"Quite the contrary. It's the best thing you could have ever done for him."

"How's that?"

"THE FEEDBACK YOU GAVE HIM WAS A GIFT. It was right on the money. He realizes that now. You highlighted exactly the kind of things he needed to say and do to win over the folks at Green Crest."

"Wow. I thought I was being a bitch, as usual."

"Hey, don't take this the wrong way. But I would have loved to have had a bitch like you as my boss in my last job. **The boss I had there only looked out after himself. When I asked him – no, begged him – for straight feedback, all I got was vague generalities like "tone down your energy" or "be less political." Stuff he couldn't define and stuff I couldn't act on. It wasn't helpful.** I think he saw me as a threat to him. That's the main reason I had to get the hell out of there."

"What a jackass! He sounds like a horrible leader."

"Absolutely! He was. And unlike him, that blunt and specific feedback you gave Drake was pitch perfect. Hey, that reminds me...let me show you something Drake gave me last night."

Clare then pulled some papers out of her purse.

"Before starting his new job, as a favor to me, I asked him to come up with some principles for managing his career going forward. I asked him to meet with some folks in my network to help him. He has been absolutely thrilled with the advice he's gotten. He said it's one of the best things he's done in his whole career."

Bursting with excitement she continued: "Check this out, Lois. He's calls it **THE NUMBER <u>ONE</u> CAREER SUCCESS SECRET.** It's kinda self-explanatory and only a few pages long. Here...take a few minutes to read through it yourself, while I visit the ladies room."

With that, she handed the papers to Lois and excused herself.

After putting on her glasses and reading through the three-page document, Lois' reaction when Clare returned was immediate, "WOW! THIS IS POWERFUL STUFF. CAN I GET A COPY?"

"Sure. But let me email it to you tomorrow. He's working on some final changes to it and I want you to have the most up to date copy."

"Okay. But please don't forget to send it. I definitely can use a copy of it for some high potential HR folks I'm coaching right now."

"I won't. In fact, he's going to give a presentation based on it to the local SHRM chapter in a couple of weeks. Why don't you come? It would be nice for you guys to catch up again."

"Sounds great, if I'm in town I will. Just email me the exact date and details."

"Will do!" Clare continued, "So you see, Drake gained a ton from you as his boss. I'm sure you can see a lot of your influence in this document he developed. He's now looking forward, not backwards. As you know, one of his goals was to be the first black VP in our company. You didn't take that away from him. You helped him. Based on your feedback and what he learned from you, he got to fulfill that dream over at Green Crest."

"Thank you for sharing all this Clare. It means a lot. I'm thrilled to hear that he is doing so well and that I was able to help him."

"Believe me, he's grateful for everything you've done."

Finally, their meals came and the two women enjoyed the rest of their dinner.

As the evening grew late, they said their goodbyes. Clare stood up and hugged Lois with tears streaming down her eyes. She embraced her with so much force that she gently tapped

Clare's shoulder and reminded her that she has this nasty little habit called breathing.

Cheeks flaming and smiling, Clare drew back and wiped the tears off of her face. She watched as Lois exited the restaurant and boarded her car to resume her exciting new life as a retiree.

On her way home that night, she couldn't wait to hold Drake in her arms. Both of their jobs were the two best gifts that she could have ever imagined. And she finally knew that Lois was the one person to thank for both of them.

When she arrived back to the condo, she saw that the bedroom light was on, and she smiled.

Good. She was glad he had waited up for her.

She dropped her purse and keys down on the kitchen counter.

She knew that she couldn't tell him everything about the conversation with Lois.

But she didn't want to.

SHE HAD EVEN BETTER NEWS.

Earlier that day she had made a visit to her doctor.

She was informed about an unexpected gift they both were about to receive.

Looking down and patting her belly, she smiled down on it just as there was a little kick inside.

Yes, there was some important news she couldn't wait to share with him.

She was sure his mom would be very pleased.

And she knew he would be too.

The End.

### # # #

P. S. True to her word, a few days later, Clare emailed to Lois a final copy of Drake's *"THE NUMBER ONE CAREER SUCCESS SECRET."* You will find it written in its entirety in next and final chapter, Chapter 33.

Enjoy!

# 33

# THE NUMBER <u>ONE</u> CAREER SUCCESS SECRET

*By Drake Williams*

**The most important HR career success secret is all about the awesome power of the number "ONE."**

**The <u>first part</u> this secret involves avoiding ONEs.** Just ONE of anything can kill your career. Specifically…

- Just ONE boss you're depending on to deliver your next promotion.
- Just ONE organization you're relying on to fulfill all your career aspirations.
- Just ONE higher up you're hoping will advocate or open doors for you.
- Just ONE mentor you're relying on as a source for great career advice.
- Just ONE direct report who is indispensable to you.
- Just ONE resume you're using for your job search.

**Just ONE of anything will LIMIT and RESTRICT your career opportunities.** In today's volatile economy, there are no guarantees. Things change in an instant. No matter how well you're doing right now, all it takes is…

- Just ONE candidate hired over your head to get you passed over for a promotion.
- Just ONE key decision-maker who decides not to support advancing you up the ladder.
- Just ONE boss who does not give good feedback...or who lacks the clout or personal interest in you to slow down the achievement of your career dreams.

So, don't allow ONEs to limit you. Instead, enlarge your options and opportunities by making...

# "ONE" HOUR PER WEEK CAREER INVESTMENTS

**This is the <u>second part</u> of this secret – the exception to the ONE rule – and the only ONE you should embrace.** It involves devoting at least <u>ONE</u> HOUR A WEEK (or 52 HOURS A YEAR) investing in actions that will enhance your ability to land future opportunities.

*This strategy is based on the fact that while performing well in your day job is absolutely vital to your success -- you should never get so busy grinding away at it, that you neglect to look up from what you're doing...to spend time on actions that can prepare you for opportunities to advance your HR career – both INSIDE and OUTSIDE of your current organization.*

These **ONE-hour per week career investments** should include time spent in any one or combination of the following:

### *Career Investment #1:* NURTURING & GROWING YOUR RELATIONSHIPS.

Regularly put time on your calendar to catch up over coffee, lunch or dinner with the 20-50 most important professional contacts in your life right now. If you can't meet them face to face, call or text them on a regular basis. Typically these are former colleagues, customers, clients, mentors or bosses…or people whose support can be valuable in your career.

These are people you don't just send a holiday cards to, these are folks you should talk to 2-3 times a year. They know you well. And you should know what their interests are too. When meeting with them, share with them you're doing. But then spend the bulk of your time finding out their issues, desires and concerns and *FIGURING OUT WAYS YOU CAN HELP THEM.* Such help is inevitably returned, even if it's not returned in the same way or in the time frame you imagined. It's called karma.

The key is to not let these relationships go cold. Keep them *warm* by networking **all the time,** even if you are happily employed or considered indispensable in your organization.

***Here's why:*** Eighty percent of all new HR opportunities surface through networking and from one's network of contacts. You never know when a sudden business change outside of your control will result in you getting passed over for the job you want or the elimination of your job. Your network of contacts is your insurance policy to cash in on when looking to identify new opportunities.

### *Career Investment #2:*
## RAISING YOUR VISIBILITY.

**This is good old fashioned face-to-face interaction.** Examples here include:

- Staying active in local networking or Meet Up groups.
- Attending SHRM meetings to broaden your exposure outside of your current organization, and volunteering at such events & joining their special committees.
- Giving talks, presentations or sharing your expertise beyond your current role so that others can benefit from and become aware of your talents.
- Raising your hand for the assignments no one wants in your current organization to expose yourself to a different group of key decision-makers.

- Finally, enhancing your visibility by using social media to supplement (not replace) "face-to-face" interactions.

*Here's why:* Getting promoted takes both *ability* and *visibility*. Flying under the radar is great for geese, but it's a horrible strategy for managing your career in HR.

## *Career Investment #3:*
## Returning All Calls From RECRUITERS, HEADHUNTERS & SEARCH FIRMS.

Call search folks back even if you're happy and not interested in a new job. Do this within 24 hours, ESPECIALLY if you can provide them with a referral for the position they're seeking.

*Here's why you want to do this:* Most HR people happy in their jobs ignore headhunter calls. If you do just the opposite, you will immediately differentiate yourself from the rest of the pack. Position yourself as someone responsive to their calls and as a *source for talent referrals.* Helping recruiters do their jobs by offering referrals is remembered and inevitably results in such generosity being returned to you. Play the long game so that when opportunities that fit you hit their screen, your name is the first one that springs to their mind. Great opportunities often arrive on your doorstep when you least expect them and search professionals can help make this happen.

## *Career Investment #4:*
## Regularly Soliciting FEEDBACK
## On How You're Doing.

Utilize formal organizational methods like 360s and feedback from your boss. In addition, seek out informal opportunities to get casual, regular one-on-one feedback from peers, former bosses or clients -- and even people outside of your organization who know you well.

*Here's why:* Advancing your career requires addressing any behavioral, skill or experience gaps you have -- and leveraging any underutilized strengths you may not be aware of. Ask others to help you better understand the gifts you have and the flat sides you need to address. Don't wait until it's too late. Consider all feedback you receive – good or bad -- as a gift. And as a gift, the appropriate response in all cases is "Thank you!"

## *Career Investment #5:*
## INCREASING YOUR VALUE.

This is done by beefing up your HR knowledge, skills and experiences by taking on developmental or "stretch" assignments to expand your capacity to assume larger roles -- or by attending seminars, workshops, webinars, conferences, reading and getting coaching from MULTIPLE MENTORS that will help you stay on the leading edge. Finally, this involves making sure your key accomplishments are always up to date on your resume and LinkedIn profile.

*Here's the rationale:* Treat yourself like a blue-chip stock. If you're not taking steps to boost your value, you are considered a stock declining in value that no one wants in their portfolio.

## Here's The Bottom Line...

**Working hard and performing well in your current job are vital...but they alone are <u>not enough</u> to ensure that you will get promoted or advance your career in HR.** To avoid getting overlooked for opportunities both inside and outside of your organization, you must embrace *"THE NUMBER <u>ONE</u> CAREER SUCCESS SECRET"* which consists of two parts:

(1) Avoiding <u>ONE</u>s. Relying exclusively on <u>ONE</u> of anything can be limiting, unforgiving and can kill your career.

(2) Instead, enlarge your career options by spending at least <u>ONE</u> HOUR a week (or 52 hours a year) making the FIVE KEY CAREER INVESTMENTS previously described. This one hour per week is the only exception to the "ONE-avoidance" rule.

###

# More Resources for Taking Your HR Career to the Next Level
*By Alan Collins*

*WINNING BIG IN HR: 100+ Powerful Strategies For Accomplishing Great Results Faster & Getting Your Clients To Rave About You As An HR Professional!*

**Available now at:**
**www.WinningBigInHR.com**

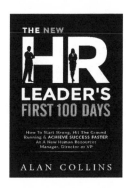

*THE NEW HR LEADER'S FIRST 100 DAYS: How To Start Strong, Hit The Ground Running & Achieve Success Faster As a New HR Manager, Director or VP.*

**Available now at:**
**www.NewHRLeader.com**

*HR INTERVIEW SECRETS: How To Ace Your Next Human Resources Interview, Dazzle Your Interviewers & Land The Job You Want!*

**Available now at:**
**www.HRInterviewSecrets.com**

# Still More Resources for Taking Your HR Career to the Next Level
*By Alan Collins*

*HR RESUME SECRETS:*
*How To Create An Irresistible Human Resources Resume That Will Open Doors, Wow Hiring Managers & Get You Interviews!*

**Available now at:**
**www.HRResumeSecrets.com**

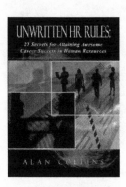

*UNWRITTEN HR RULES:*
*21 Secrets for Attaining Awesome Career Success in Human Resources*

**Available now at:**
**www.UnwrittenHRRules.com**

*BEST KEPT HR SECRETS:*
*400 Most Powerful Tips For Thriving At Work, Making Yourself Indispensable & Attaining Outrageous Success in Human Resources*

**Available now at:**
**www.BestKeptHRSecrets.com**

# ABOUT THE AUTHORS

**ALAN L. COLLINS** is Founder of *Success in HR* and helps human resources professionals around the globe accelerate their career success. He is the author of ten books including the Amazon best sellers *Unwritten HR Rules, HR Interview Secrets* and *The New HR Leader's First 100 Days*. He was formerly vice president of HR at PepsiCo where he led talent and human resources initiatives for the Quaker Oats, Gatorade and Tropicana businesses.

**ALLISON P. QUINN** is a novelist and fiction writer of entertaining stories about finding success and meaning in the workplace. All of her stories are quick reads which help professionals in today's organizations succeed. She specializes in infusing her tales with workplace romance, mystery and intrigue to carry the reader on a journey of discovery towards realizing that ONE, single golden nugget of wisdom she has waiting at the end of her stories.